The fantastic freestanding

FLiP
QUIZ

2nd–4th Grade

General Knowledge

Silver Dolphin Books
An imprint of the Advantage Publishers Group
5880 Oberlin Drive, San Diego, CA 92121-4794
www.advantagebooksonline.com

First published in 2001 by Miles Kelly Publishing Ltd
Bardfield Centre, Great Bardfield, Essex, CM7 4SL

ISBN 1-57145-808-5

1 2 3 4 5 06 05 04 03 02

Questions compiled by John Paton, Brian Williams and Andy Langley
Editors: Kate Miles, Rosie Alexander
Picture research: Liberty Newton
Artwork commissioning: Lesley Cartlidge
Design: Joe Jones
Cover design: Clare Sleven
Illustrations: Martin Camm, Mike Foster/Maltings Partnership, Jeremy Gower,
Richard Hook, Rob Jakeway, Steve Kirk, Steve Lings/Linden Artists, Rob McCaig,
Josephine Martin, Gill Platt, Terry Riley, Eric Rowe/Linden Artists, Mike Saunders,
Peter Sarson, Don Simpson/Specs Art, Guy Smith/Mainline Design,
Roger Smith, Colin Woolf
Photographs: MKP Archive and Corbis
Color reproduction: DPI Colour Ltd

Printed in Thailand

KEY TO SYMBOLS

$\sqrt{x}$	Math		People in History
	Science & Technology		Inventions & Machines
	Human Body		Exploration & Discovery
	Natural World		Warfare & Weapons
	Scientists at Work		The Arts
	Earth & Space		English Language
	Geography	?	General Knowledge
	History		

You will find more than 1000 questions in this book. If you are answering questions on your own, just cover the answers with your hand or a piece of paper. You may want to write down your answers and count up your scores for each quiz.

If you are doing the quizzes with a partner or in teams, unfold the base and stand the Flip Quiz on a flat surface between you and your partner. Read the questions aloud (but not the answers!) and allow your partner to say the answers or write them down. You may answer each question in turn or answer an entire quiz in turn. Keep your scores on a piece of paper and compare results.

The illustrations are there to help you get the right answers when competing with a partner. For instance, if you are answering Quiz 1 questions, you will be looking at and reading out Quiz 2. However, the illustrations you see are clues to help you do Quiz 1. Look at the labels by the illustrations. These tell you which question they are clues for. The pictures behind the quiz numbers at the top of the page are not such obvious clues, but they may still help you get an answer.

The questions are divided into fifteen subjects: Math, Science & Technology, Human Body, Natural World, Scientists at Work, Earth & Space, Geography, History, People in History, Inventions & Machines, Exploration & Discovery, Warfare & Weapons, The Arts, English Language, and General Knowledge.

As you progress through the quizzes, you will notice that the questions get a little harder. We think the easiest level is Level 1 and the hardest is Level 3, but you may find it the other way around. It all depends on what you happen to know.

Levels
There are three levels of questions; they get harder as you progress.

Question categories
The questions are divided into 15 subjects (see key above).

Picture clues 1
These visual clues are not always obvious (and they don't have labels).

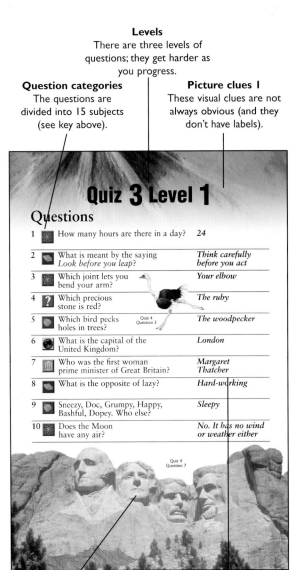

Quiz 3 Level 1

Questions

1		How many hours are there in a day?	*24*
2		What is meant by the saying *Look before you leap?*	*Think carefully before you act*
3		Which joint lets you bend your arm?	*Your elbow*
4	?	Which precious stone is red?	*The ruby*
5		Which bird pecks holes in trees?	*The woodpecker*
6		What is the capital of the United Kingdom?	*London*
7		Who was the first woman prime minister of Great Britain?	*Margaret Thatcher*
8		What is the opposite of lazy?	*Hard-working*
9		Sneezy, Doc, Grumpy, Happy, Bashful, Dopey. Who else?	*Sleepy*
10		Does the Moon have any air?	*No. It has no wind or weather either*

Quiz 4 Question 3

Quiz 4 Question 7

Picture clues 2
These visual clues will often help you get the answer; the label tells you which question they refer to.

Answers
When doing the quizzes on your own, cover the answers with your hand or a piece of paper.

Quiz 1 Level 1

Questions	Answers
1 What are the Himalayas, the Alps, and the Pyrenees examples of?	Mountain ranges
2 Which is the biggest land animal?	The African elephant
3 What is the opposite of *above*?	Below
4 Where is the Antarctic?	At the South Pole
5 Is the Sun a star?	Yes
6 Who was Cleopatra?	The last queen of Egypt
7 What does *to lose your nerve* mean?	To become afraid
8 What is an igloo?	An Inuit house built of ice blocks
9 In which city would you find Central Park?	New York
10 What shape has three sides?	A triangle

Quiz 2
Question 10

Quiz 2
Question 6

Quiz 2 Level 1

Questions	Answers
1 Are all snakes poisonous?	*No*
2 What is an iceberg?	*A large block of ice that floats in the sea*
3 What is *in the nick of time*?	*At the last possible moment*
4 Which came first, the Stone Age or the Bronze Age?	*The Stone Age*
5 What is the world's biggest ocean?	*The Pacific*
6 Which red fruit is famously eaten at the Wimbledon tennis championships?	*The strawberry*
7 Which black and white striped animal looks like the horse?	*The zebra*
8 What do we call the U-shaped plate nailed to a horse's hoof?	*A horseshoe*
9 Does the Earth travel around the Sun?	*Yes (it takes a year)*
10 Which bear has a white coat?	*The polar bear*

Quiz I
Question 2

Quiz I
Question 8

Quiz 3 Level 1

Questions		Answers
1	How many hours are there in a day?	24
2	What is meant by the saying *Look before you leap*?	*Think carefully before you act*
3	Which joint lets you bend your arm?	*Your elbow*
4	Which precious stone is red?	*The ruby*
5	Which bird pecks holes in trees?	*The woodpecker*
6	What is the capital of the United Kingdom?	*London*
7	Who was the first woman prime minister of Great Britain?	*Margaret Thatcher*
8	What is the opposite of lazy?	*Hard-working*
9	Sneezy, Doc, Grumpy, Happy, Bashful, Dopey. Who else?	*Sleepy*
10	Does the Moon have any air?	*No. It has no wind or weather either*

Quiz 4
Question 3

Quiz 4
Question 7

Quiz 4 Level 1

Questions | Answers

#	Question	Answer
1	Who was the German leader during World War II?	*Adolf Hitler*
2	What is the world's highest mountain?	*Mount Everest 29,028 feet (8,848 m)*
3	What is the largest bird?	*The ostrich*
4	What is the capital of France?	*Paris*
5	What is meant by the saying *Many hands make light work*?	*If a task is shared by many, it is easier*
6	Where are your taste buds?	*On your tongue*
7	Heads of U.S. Presidents are carved into which mountain?	*Mount Rushmore*
8	Which saint is Santa Claus named for?	*St. Nicholas*
9	What is the rough outside of a tree called?	*The bark*
10	What was Cinderella's coach made from?	*A pumpkin*

Quiz 3
Question 7

Quiz 3
Question 5

Quiz 5 Level 1

Questions | Answers

		Questions	Answers
1	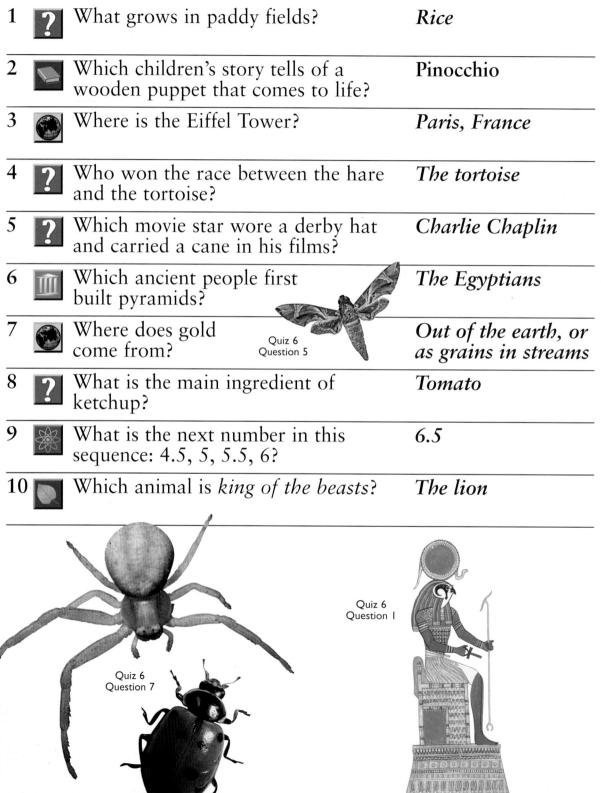	What grows in paddy fields?	*Rice*
2		Which children's story tells of a wooden puppet that comes to life?	**Pinocchio**
3		Where is the Eiffel Tower?	*Paris, France*
4		Who won the race between the hare and the tortoise?	*The tortoise*
5		Which movie star wore a derby hat and carried a cane in his films?	*Charlie Chaplin*
6		Which ancient people first built pyramids?	*The Egyptians*
7		Where does gold come from?	*Out of the earth, or as grains in streams*
8		What is the main ingredient of ketchup?	*Tomato*
9		What is the next number in this sequence: 4.5, 5, 5.5, 6?	6.5
10		Which animal is *king of the beasts*?	*The lion*

Quiz 6
Question 5

Quiz 6
Question 1

Quiz 6
Question 7

Quiz **6** Level **1**

Questions

Answers

1. Which god did the Egyptians believe was swallowed by the sky goddess Nut? — *The sun god Ra*

2. What is a tam-ó-shanter? — *A flat-topped cap*

3. In which state are the Everglades? — *Florida*

4. Complete this saying: *As dry as a...* — *Bone*

5. What does a caterpillar turn into? — *A butterfly or a moth*

6. Which sport is associated with Wimbledon? — *Tennis*

7. Is a spider an insect? — *No (insects have 6 legs, spiders have 8)*

8. Do camels store water in their humps? — *No (their humps are full of fat)*

9. Which parts of the Earth have the longest summer days? — *The North and South Poles*

10. What do we use our lungs for? — *Breathing*

Quiz 5
Question 8

Quiz 5
Question 10

Quiz 5
Question 2

Quiz 7 Level 1

	Questions	Answers
1	What is the opposite of soft?	*Hard*
2	In which sea does the island of Malta lie?	*The Mediterranean Sea*
3	Which sport uses a puck?	*Ice hockey*
4	Which girl walked along the Yellow Brick Road?	*Dorothy in* The Wizard of Oz
5	Where does a mole live?	*Under the ground*
6	Which is the Earth's only natural satellite?	*The Moon*
7	What is the capital of Russia?	*Moscow*
8	Which bear did A.A. Milne write about?	*Winnie the Pooh*
9	What is a young cow called?	*A calf*
10	Do all birds fly?	*No. Penguins, kiwis, and ostriches do not*

Quiz 8
Question 6

Quiz 8
Question 1

Quiz 8 Level 1

	Questions	Answers
1	Which country does spaghetti come from?	*Italy*
2	In which country does the emu live?	*Australia*
3	What frightened Miss Muffet away?	*A spider*
4	What are car tires made of?	*Rubber*
5	What was Cinderella's slipper made of?	*Glass*
6	Which bird is the symbol of peace?	*The dove*
7	What are cappuccino and espresso?	*Coffee drinks*
8	Where was the first Thanksgiving meal?	*Plymouth, Massachusetts*
9	What is a young horse called?	*A foal*
10	What is the stern of a ship?	*The back*

Quiz 7
Question 6

Quiz 7
Question 9

Quiz 9 Level 1

Questions	Answers

1 ❓ What is made from chocolate at Easter?   *Easter eggs and Easter bunnies*

2 ⚛️ What sort of creature was a *Diplodocus*?   *A dinosaur*

3 ❓ Who was the religious member of Robin Hood's band?   *Friar Tuck*

4 📙 Who wrote *The Ugly Duckling*?   *Hans Christian Andersen*

5 ❓ What is caught in pots in the sea?   *Lobsters and crabs*

6 🍃 Which is the smallest breed of dog?   *The chihuahua*

7 🌐 Which country names its years after animals?   *China*

8 ❓ Which international sporting event took place in Barcelona, Spain, 1992?   *The Summer Olympics*

9 🏛️ What was the name of the rebel southern states in the Civil War?   *The Confederacy*

10 ⚛️ What is 21 + 0?   *21*

Quiz 10
Question 1

Quiz 10
Question 4

Quiz 10 Level 1

Questions	Answers
1 Who did Simple Simon meet on his way to the fair?	*A pieman*
2 What is a hurricane?	*A storm with very strong winds*
3 How many sides does a hexagon have?	*6*
4 What are young ducks called?	*Ducklings*
5 Who wrote *Rip Van Winkle*?	*Washington Irving*
6 Are any two fingerprints the same?	*No, not even those of identical twins*
7 What is insomnia?	*An inability to sleep*
8 Around which sea was the Roman empire formed?	*The Mediterranean Sea*
9 What is the Muslim holy book called?	*The Koran*
10 What makes your pulse beat?	*Your heart pumping blood*

Quiz 9
Question 6

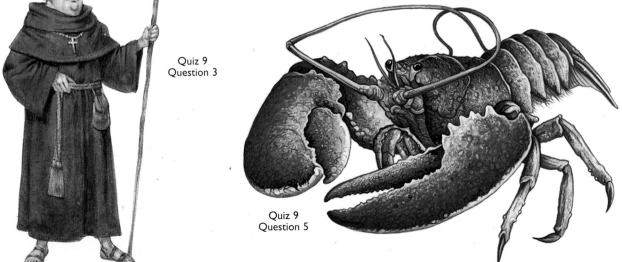

Quiz 9
Question 3

Quiz 9
Question 5

Quiz 11 Level 1

Questions	Answers
1. Which is the world's biggest desert?	*The Sahara in Africa*
2. What are the Wright brothers famous for?	*They flew the first powered airplane*
3. Shot put, pole vault, and javelin are examples of what?	*Track and field sports*
4. Who said: *Elementary, my dear Watson?*	*Sherlock Holmes*
5. What is the ingredient that makes bread rise?	*Yeast*
6. What color was the owl and the pussycat's boat?	*Pea green*
7. Which ancient civilization grew up around the river Nile?	*The Egyptian civilization*
8. Which vegetable has a big orange-red root?	*The carrot*
9. What are your milk teeth?	*The first set of teeth you get as a baby*
10. How many days are there in a year?	*Normally 365, 366 in a leap year*

Quiz 12
Question 4

Quiz 12
Question 2

Quiz 12 Level 1

Questions	Answers
1 Where is the kimono worn?	In Japan
2 What types of coin would you associate with pirates?	Pieces of eight
3 In which town was Jesus born?	Bethlehem
4 Which fish looks like a snake?	An eel
5 What is a female fox called?	A vixen
6 Where is the Empire State Building?	New York City
7 What is 54 – 0?	54
8 Which is the Lone Star State?	Texas
9 What does an elephant use for smelling and lifting things?	Its trunk
10 What is the plural of roof?	Roofs

Quiz 11
Question 8

Quiz 11
Question 6

Quiz 11
Question 4

Quiz 13 Level 1

Questions

Answers

1	Was it Edison or Faraday who invented the light bulb?	*Edison*
2	What did Henry Ford make in his factories?	*Cars*
3	Were tea bags invented in the 1740s or the 1920s?	*The 1920s*
4	The Battle of Hastings is recorded on which famous tapestry?	*The Bayeux Tapestry*
5	In which sport was Ty Cobb a star?	*Baseball*
6	How did Sir Humphry Davy make coal mining safer?	*He invented a miner's safety lamp*
7	Which industry was revolutionized by the invention of the flying shuttle: weaving, shipping, or mining?	*Weaving*
8	What did the ancient Egyptians use to sweeten food before the discovery of sugar?	*Honey*
9	What was Margot Fonteyn famous for: dancing, acting, or singing?	*Dancing*
10	Which actor played James Bond in the first Bond film?	*Sean Connery*

Quiz 14
Question 8

Quiz 14
Question 9

Quiz 14
Question 3

Quiz 14 Level 1

Questions

Answers

		Question	Answer
1		Which people first brought the cat to Europe?	*The Romans*
2		In which war were the battles of Bull Run and Gettysburg?	*American Civil War*
3		Who was the first British monarch to travel in a train?	*Queen Victoria*
4		In which World War did poet Wilfred Owen fight?	*World War I*
5		Which Disney movie was based on a novel by French writer Victor Hugo?	**The Hunchback of Notre Dame**
6		Where does the expression "checkmate" in chess come from?	*Arabic "shah mat", "the king is dead."*
7		Roughly how many stone slabs are there in the Great Pyramid: 2,000, 20,000, or 2 million?	*2 million*
8		What is the arrow of a crossbow called?	*A bolt*
9		In which country did Ned Kelly become an outlaw?	*Australia*
10		What was special about the Heinkel He-178 plane, first flown in 1939?	*It was the first jet plane to fly*

Quiz 13
Question 6

Quiz 13, Question 4

Quiz 15 Level 1

Questions

Answers

		Question	Answer
1		Who were the first people to live in Australia?	*The Aborigines*
2		Which prince led the English to victory at Crécy in 1346?	*The Black Prince*
3		Whom did Anne of Cleves and Anne Boleyn marry?	*King Henry VIII*
4		Was Holbein a famous painter, musician, or general?	*Painter*
5		Where did a cowboy wear his chaps?	*On his legs*
6		What did a Hungarian named Biro invent in the 1940s?	*The ballpoint pen*
7		What sort of structures did the Incas build to worship their gods?	*Pyramids or ziggurats*
8		By what nickname was U.S. astronaut Edwin Aldrin known?	*Buzz*
9		What did Krakatoa do in 1883?	*It blew up: it was a volcano*
10		What is a long barrow?	*A kind of Stone Age grave*

Quiz 16
Question 1

Quiz 16
Question 10

Quiz 16
Question 6

Quiz 16 Level 1

Questions

Answers

		Questions	Answers
1	?	What name was given to the Celtic priests?	*Druids*
2		What kind of letters made up the Viking alphabet?	*Runes*
3		What did a man named Dunlop invent in the 1880s?	*The air-filled tire*
4	?	Who is the only English king called "the Great"?	*Alfred the Great*
5		With what is the inventor Charles Babbage linked: computers, medicine, or balloons?	*Computers*
6		Who recorded a best-selling album called *Thriller?*	*Michael Jackson*
7		Who were the first people to make paper?	*The Chinese*
8		Was dynamite an explosive or an early plastic?	*An explosive, invented in 1866*
9		Who returned to space in 1998 at the age of 77?	*John Glen*
10		Which empire was conquered by Pizarro?	*The Inca empire*

Quiz 15
Question 6

Quiz 15
Question 7

Quiz 17 Level 1

Questions

Answers

		Question	Answer
1	?	Which musical instrument was invented by Adolphe Saxe?	*The saxophone*
2		Which explorer was first to reach the South Pole?	*Roald Amundsen*
3		What is an abacus used for?	*Mathematical calculations*
4		What was the name of the fleet sent by Spain against England in 1588?	*The Armada*
5		Which country used to be led by rulers called czars?	*Russia*
6		In which foreign wars did King Richard I of England go to fight?	*The Crusades*
7		What do we call the ancient form of decoration using small pieces of tile or stone?	*Mosaic*
8	?	In which British castle would you find Beefeaters?	*The Tower of London*
9	?	In which year were the very first Olympic games held: 776BC, AD776, or AD1000?	*776BC*
10		What event do the French people celebrate on July 14?	*The fall of the Bastille*

Quiz 18
Question 3

Quiz 18
Question 2

Quiz 18 Level 1

Questions

Answers

1		Which began first: the French Revolution or the American Revolution?	*The American (in 1775)*
2		How many wheels did a Celtic war chariot have?	*Two*
3		What kind of boats did Polynesians use for ocean voyages?	*Outrigger canoes*
4		Which Greek philosopher lived in a barrel?	*Diogenes*
5		Of which people was Genghis Khan a war leader?	*The Mongols*
6		In Shakespeare's play, who is the boy Juliet falls in love with?	*Romeo*
7		In which country did the ancient Olmecs live?	*Mexico*
8		Between which two countries does Offa's Dyke run?	*England and Wales*
9		Which Polish astronomer shocked people by saying that the Earth was not the center of the Universe?	*Copernicus*
10		After which Greek victory in 490BC did a messenger run 26 miles to announce the news?	*Marathon*

Quiz 17
Question 1

Quiz 17
Question 2

Quiz 17
Question 4

Quiz 19 Level 1

	Questions	Answers
1	With which queen did Julius Caesar and Mark Antony fall in love?	*Cleopatra*
2	It was once called Byzantium and then Constantinople. What do we call this city today?	*Istanbul*
3	What was Einstein's first name?	*Albert*
4	Was an autogyro an early helicopter-like plane or an early computer?	*An early helicopter-like plane*
5	Who was the ruler of the Greek gods?	*Zeus*
6	What kind of weapon was a tomahawk?	*An ax*
7	What was the name of the first jet airliner to fly?	*Comet*
8	Which came first: clay pots or metal tools?	*Clay pots*
9	Who wrote *Oliver Twist*?	*Charles Dickens*
10	Which material was accidentally made by ancient Egyptians when they lit a fire on a beach?	*Glass*

Quiz 20
Question 1

Quiz 20
Question 3

Quiz 20
Question 8

Quiz 20 Level 1

Questions

Answers

		Questions	Answers
1		What was DDT invented to do?	*Kill insect pests*
2		What were the Crusades?	*Religious wars against the Turks*
3		Where did Vasco da Gama sail in 1498?	*India*
4		Who commanded the British fleet at the Battle of Trafalgar in 1805?	*Nelson*
5		Which country built the *Nautilus*, the world's first nuclear submarine?	*The United States*
6		In which wars did the families of York and Lancaster fight each other?	*The Wars of the Roses*
7		Who was the second president of the United States?	*John Adams*
8		The people of which "classical" empire worshipped the goddess Athene: Greece or Rome?	*Greece*
9		In the Bible, who built the Ark to save his family and the animals from the flood?	*Noah*
10		Which country developed the TGV high speed train?	*France*

Quiz 19
Question 4

Quiz 19
Question 1

Quiz 19
Question 9

Quiz 21 Level 1

Questions

Answers

#	Question	Answer
1	Was a clipper a fast sailing ship, a surgical instrument, or a racehorse?	*A sailing ship*
2	Which branch of mathematics is named after the Arabic word *al-jabr*, to reduce?	*Algebra*
3	Who was the Greek slave who wrote the first animal fables in about 570BC?	*Aesop*
4	Who was the first man to orbit the Earth in a spacecraft?	*Yuri Gagarin (in 1961)*
5	When did people first use electric toasters: 1880s or 1920s?	*1920s*
6	What do the smiling and sad theater masks stand for?	*Comedy and tragedy*
7	Which was the last to be used in Europe: knife, fork, or spoon?	*Fork*
8	Was a minuet an old-fashioned dance, a gun, or an early clock?	*An old-fashioned dance*
9	Odin was the chief god of which race of people?	*Vikings, or Norsemen*
10	What is the ancient Egyptian form of writing called?	*Hieroglyphics*

Quiz 22
Question 5

Quiz 22
Question 7

Quiz 22 Level 1

	Questions	Answers
1	Which boxer said "I am the Greatest"?	*Muhammad Ali*
2	Which two countries fought the Hundred Years' War?	*England and France*
3	According to legend, which Irish saint sailed to America in a leather boat in AD860?	*Brendan*
4	In which century was the French Revolution: 15th, 17th, or 18th?	*18th century*
5	Which came first: electric street lights or gas lamps?	*Gas lamps*
6	What instruments did the Chinese use to pull out rotten teeth?	*Their fingers!*
7	Which sort of men used to joust on horses?	*Knights*
8	On which Mediterranean island was Napoleon Bonaparte born?	*Corsica*
9	Which Scottish inventor pioneered the television?	*John Logie Baird*
10	Which famous artist wrote in mirror writing (back to front)?	*Leonardo da Vinci*

Quiz 21
Question 9

Quiz 21
Question 10

Quiz 23 Level 1

Questions

Answers

		Questions	Answers
1		Which countries developed the *Concorde*?	*The UK and France*
2		Which empire was ruled by Darius the Great?	*The Persian Empire*
3		Who was the most famous escape artist of the 20th century?	*Harry Houdini*
4		What did Alexander Graham Bell invent in 1877?	*The telephone*
5		In which century did people first travel in cars?	*19th*
6		James Hargreaves invented the spinning jenny to do which job?	*Spin wool into yarn*
7		What did Volta invent in 1800?	*The electric battery*
8		Which U.S. president was elected in 1976?	*Jimmy Carter*
9		Which state in ancient Greece forced its people to live a strict life without any luxuries?	*Sparta*
10		In which sport did Jack Nicklaus find fame and fortune?	*Golf*

Quiz 24
Question 4

Quiz 24
Question 3

Quiz 24
Question 8

Questions

Answers

		Questions	Answers
1		What was special about the British ship *Dreadnought* of 1906?	*It was the first modern battleship*
2		What was the painter Picasso's first name?	*Pablo*
3		Who was Queen of England at the time of the Spanish Armada?	*Queen Elizabeth I*
4		What kind of warplane is a B-52?	*A long-range bomber, used by the US Air Force*
5		Which fast food gets its name from a city in Germany?	*Hamburger (from Hamburg)*
6		Of which revolution was Robespierre a leader?	*The French Revolution*
7		Who was Robin Hood's sweetheart?	*Maid Marian*
8		What was a boneshaker?	*An early bicycle*
9		Who is the father of Britain's princes William and Harry?	*Charles, Prince of Wales*
10		In which sport was Pelé an international star?	*Soccer*

Quiz 23
Question 10

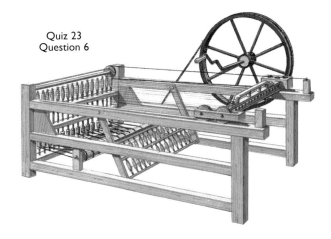

Quiz 23
Question 6

Quiz 23
Question 2

Quiz 25 Level 1

Questions

Answers

		Questions	Answers
1		Which one of the world's most important inventions was first used about 5,500 years ago?	*The wheel*
2		What is the nearest star to Earth?	*The Sun*
3	$\sqrt{x}$	What is a straight line on a piece of paper, that goes from side to side?	*A horizontal line*
4		What does a mathematician study?	*Numbers*
5		What is the nearest object in space to Earth?	*The Moon*
6	$\sqrt{x}$	How many points does a star have?	*5*
7		What is used to color cloth?	*Dye*
8		What part of your body do you think with?	*Your brain*
9		When a sound bounces off something such as a wall what do you hear?	*An echo*
10		Where do you go for an operation or if you are hurt?	*Hospital*

Quiz 26
Question 5

Quiz 26
Question 7

Quiz 26
Question 1

Quiz 26 Level 1

Questions

Answers

#		Question	Answer
1		What would help you float safely to the ground from an airplane?	*A parachute*
2		Could we live on any other planet apart from Earth?	*No*
3		What shape is a cereal box?	*A cuboid*
4		What forms over a cut when it is healing?	*A scab*
5		What does the word magnify in magnifying glass mean?	*Make bigger*
6		Which two parts of your body do you brush each day?	*Your hair and teeth*
7		How do you produce a sound from a wind instrument?	*By blowing into it*
8		What must an astronaut wear in space?	*A spacesuit*
9		What is half of 48?	*24*
10		What happens to butter when it is heated?	*It melts*

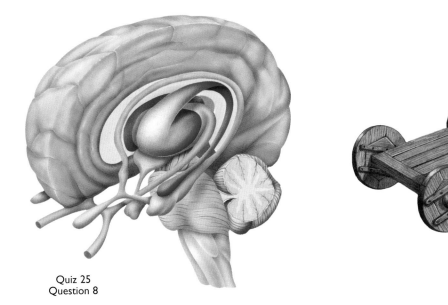

Quiz 25
Question 1

Quiz 25
Question 8

Quiz 27 Level 1

Questions

Answers

		Questions	Answers
1	$\sqrt{x}$	Which shape has 3 sides and 3 corners?	A triangle
2		Why do we only see stars at night?	Because sunlight is brighter than starlight
3		What covers your whole body?	Your skin
4		The shape of a rainbow is a circle. True or false?	True
5		Who looks after your teeth?	A dentist
6		Is your heart above or below your stomach?	Above
7		What gives a car energy to work?	Gasoline or diesel
8	$\sqrt{x}$	How many corners does a rectangle have?	Four
9		What is the name for a boat that travels underwater?	A submarine
10	$\sqrt{x}$	How many fives in 45?	9

Quiz 28
Question 7

Quiz 28
Question 10

Quiz 28 Level 1

Questions

Answers

1		What part of your body do you see with?		*Your eyes*
2		Which do we hear or see first, thunder or lightning?		*Lightning*
3		Which shape has four sides the same length?		*A square*
4		What disease makes you sneeze and your nose run?		*A cold*
5		What is 100 ÷ 10?		*10*
6		What work does a surgeon do?	Quiz 27 Question 6	*Carries out operations*
7		What is put in a flashlight to give it the power to work?		*A battery*
8		How many hours are there in a day?		*24*
9		What are dairy products made from?		*Milk*
10		Which toy is the oldest flying machine?		*A kite*

Quiz 27
Question 9

Quiz 29 Level 1

Questions

		Questions	Answers
1		What shape is a planet?	A sphere
2		Which tool has a toothed blade for cutting?	A saw
3		What nationality was Galileo— English, Greek, or Italian?	Italian
4		What gives a yacht the power to move?	Wind
5		How many centimeters in a meter?	100
6		What part of your body do you taste with?	Your tongue
7		What is 20 x 0?	0
8		What kind of doctor treats animals?	Veterinarian
9		What always covers the top of a tall mountain?	Snow and ice
10		What do we call the invisible mixture of gases all around us?	Air

Quiz 30
Question 10

Quiz 30
Question 8

Quiz 30
Question 6

Quiz 30 Level 1

Questions

Answers

1		What is solid water called?	*Ice*
2		Which star gives Earth its heat and light?	*The Sun*
3		Are more people left or right handed?	*Right handed*
4		How many minutes until midday if the time is 11:15 am?	*45*
5		Which will float in water: a cork, a nail, or a coin?	*A cork*
6		Which tool is used to push in and pull out nails?	*A hammer*
7		What is an island surrounded by?	*Water*
8		What part of your body do you hear with?	*Your ears*
9		What natural material is paper made from?	*Wood*
10		Which shape has six square faces?	*A cube*

Quiz 29
Question 1

Quiz 29
Question 6

Quiz 29
Question 8

Quiz 31 Level 1

Questions

Answers

		Questions	Answers
1	$\sqrt{x}$	How many legs do 10 ants have?	60
2		What do you do to an egg to boil it?	Cook it in hot water
3		What are formed when wind blows over the sea?	Waves
4		You can feel with your hair. True or false?	False
5		What do you see when you look in a mirror?	A reflection
6		Is Earth a star or a planet?	A planet
7	$\sqrt{x}$	What instrument is used to draw and measure straight lines?	A ruler
8	$\sqrt{x}$	Which is shorter, 1 3/4 miles or 1.5 miles?	1.5 miles
9		Which machine is controlled by a mouse?	A computer
10		Do shiny things feel rough or smooth?	Smooth

Quiz 32
Question 5

Quiz 32 Level 1

Questions

Answers

#		Question	Answer
1		What is the name for a space traveler?	*Astronaut*
2		What is double 30?	*60*
3		What is the name of the liquid that pours from a volcano?	*Lava*
4		How many sides does a parallelogram have?	*Four*
5		What has a seat, pedals, and a chain?	*A bicycle*
6		What are the primary colors?	*Red, yellow, and blue*
7		What does invisible mean?	*You can't see it*
8		What is the Sun made of?	*Burning gas*
9		What cylinder is used in pastry making?	*A rolling pin*
10		What is the total of 9, 9, and 9?	*27*

Quiz 31
Question 9

Quiz 31
Question 6

Quiz 33 Level 1

Questions   ## Answers

1	What can we measure in liters and milliliters?	*Liquid*
2	What part of your body do you smell with?	*Your nose*
3	What covers more of the Earth: land or sea?	*Sea*
4	Which numbers show on a digital clock at midnight?	*12:00*
5	What is formed when a river flows over a cliff?	*A waterfall*
6	What do we usually call an omnibus?	*A bus*
7	What kind of energy comes into houses through wires?	*Electricity*
8	Which of these shapes would not roll—cylinder, sphere, cuboid?	*A cuboid*
9	What black powder is swept from chimneys?	*Soot*
10	What vehicle rushes emergency patients to hospital?	*An ambulance*

Quiz 34
Question 1

Quiz 34
Question 8

Quiz  34 Level 1

Questions

Answers

		Questions	Answers
1		What part of your body has a palm?	*Your hand*
2		What food is made from cocoa beans?	*Chocolate*
3		What is the name for a building where things are made?	*A factory*
4		What part of a mountain is the peak?	*The very top*
5		What do you have tested when you go to the optician?	*Your eyes*
6		What should you do before you eat or drink?	*Wash your hands*
7		What are the straight lines light travels in called?	*Rays*
8		Which instrument do we use to measure time?	*A clock*
9		What does water become when it boils?	*Steam*
10		What is the missing number—2, 4, ?, 8, 10?	*6*

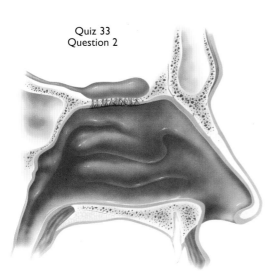

Quiz 33
Question 2

Quiz 33
Question 5

Quiz 35 Level 1

Questions

Answers

		Questions	Answers
1		How is seawater different from fresh water?	It's salty
2	√x	In which direction does a compass needle point?	North
3	√x	How many hours are there between 10:30 am and 4:30 pm?	Six
4		What kind of fuel is cut from underground mines?	Coal
5		What happens to your face when you blush?	It turns red
6		What is raw food?	Uncooked food
7		How many lungs do you have?	Two
8		Which are the two coldest places on Earth?	The North and South Poles
9		What is made when light cannot shine through a solid object?	A shadow
10	√x	A right angle is how many degrees?	90

Quiz 36
Question 6

Quiz 36
Question 1

Quiz 36 Level 1

Questions

Answers

		Question	Answer
1		Which machine keeps food cool?	*A refrigerator*
2		Which season brings the warmest weather?	*Summer*
3		Which will fit together with no spaces in between—circles or squares?	*Squares*
4		How do you produce a sound from a drum?	*By hitting it*
5		How many centimeters in half a meter?	*50*
6		What part of your body do you feel with?	*Your skin*
7		What do you find out when you measure how heavy you are ?	*Your weight*
8		What shape is like a ball?	*A sphere*
9		How many days are there in September?	*30*
10		Where would you find your nostrils?	*Your nose*

Quiz 35
Question 4

Quiz 35
Question 2

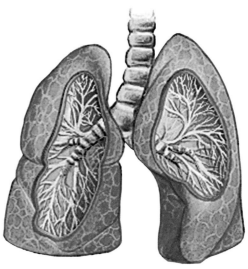

Quiz 35
Question 7

Quiz 37 Level 2

Questions

Answers

1.  What is cutlery? — *Knives, forks, and spoons*

2. When we serve a drink *on the rocks* what do we mean? — *It is served with ice*

3. Which sub-group of animals do mice, rats, and squirrels belong to? — *Rodents*

4. Are there mountains under the ocean? — *Yes*

5. Who spent three days inside a whale? — *Jonah*

6. Does wood float? — *Yes*

7. What are tributaries? — *Streams feeding into a large river*

8. What did Alexander Graham Bell invent in 1876? — *The telephone*

9. What is a young bear called? — *A cub*

10. How high is a basketball hoop? — *Ten feet (3 m)*

Quiz 38
Question 5

Quiz 38
Question I

Quiz 38
Question 3

Quiz 38 Level 2

Questions

Answers

1. What cathedral in London was designed by Sir Christopher Wren? — *St. Paul's Cathedral*

2. What is the capital of Greece? — *Athens*

3. Which rabbit-like animal has long ears and long back legs? — *The hare*

4. Do lines of latitude run north and south or east and west? — *East and west*

5. In *The Wizard of Oz*, which character was looking for a heart? — *The Tin Man*

6. Which mountain did Edmund Hillary climb in 1953? — *Mount Everest*

7. What keeps a hovercraft up? — *A cushion of air*

8. In which sport do people use pommel horses and parallel bars? — *Gymnastics*

9. What is the word *flu* short for? — *Influenza*

10. How does the kangaroo move along at speed? — *By taking large leaps*

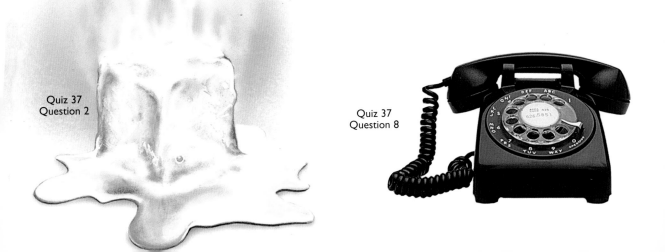

Quiz 37
Question 2

Quiz 37
Question 8

Quiz 39 Level 2

Questions

Answers

1. How many cards are in a deck? — **52**

2. What form of transportation does a cavalry regiment use? — *Horses*

3. Where does the Pope live? — *In Vatican City*

4. Which snake makes a noise with its tail? — *The rattlesnake*

5. Which canal links the Red Sea with the Mediterranean? — *The Suez Canal*

6. Where did little Jack Horner sit? — *In the corner*

7. You can see through it and it's made from sand. What is it? — *Glass*

8. Which creature has a sting in its tail? — *The scorpion*

9. Who was the Maid of Orléans? — *Joan of Arc*

10. What does a stitch in time save? — *9 (stitches)*

Quiz 40
Question 6

Quiz 40
Question 3

Quiz 40 Level 2

Questions	Answers
1. What does *keep your nose clean* mean?	*Keep out of trouble*
2. Which part of the body do you use for hearing and balancing?	*Your ears*
3. According to the Christmas carol, which bird is in the pear tree?	*A partridge*
4. Where is the Statue of Liberty?	*On an island in New York Harbor*
5. What was a legionary?	*A Roman soldier*
6. Which animal do they herd in Lapland?	*The reindeer*
7. Which girl's grandmother was eaten by a wolf?	*Little Red Riding Hood*
8. Who created Mickey Mouse and Donald Duck?	*Walt Disney*
9. What shape is a sphere?	*Ball-shaped*
10. What is 5½ as a decimal?	*5.5*

Quiz 39
Question 9

Quiz 39
Question 8

Quiz 41 Level 2

Questions	Answers
1 What is a noun?	*A person, place, or thing*
2 Which brass instrument has a sliding section?	*The trombone*
3 What is the capital of Northern Ireland?	*Belfast*
4 What is created when a meteorite hits a planet?	*A crater*
5 What do we do when we have a nap?	*Have a short sleep*
6 What did David use to kill Goliath?	*A stone in a sling*
7 Why do you sneeze?	*To clear something from your nose*
8 Which was the biggest dinosaur?	**Brachiosaurus**
9 Which bird has big, round eyes at the front of its head?	*The owl*
10 What is another name for the Netherlands?	*Holland*

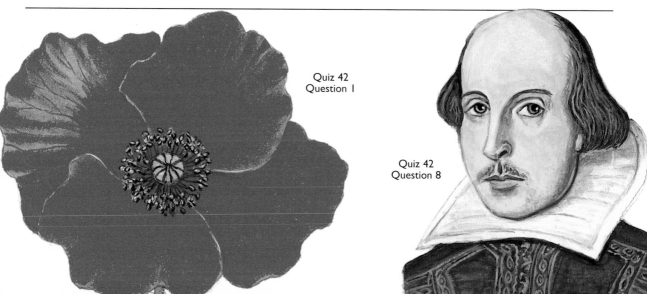

Quiz 42
Question 1

Quiz 42
Question 8

Quiz 42 Level 2

Questions	Answers

Questions   **Answers**

1　Which flower commemorates the war dead? — *The poppy*

2　What is another word for *begin*? — *Start or commence*

3　How many bones are in the human body? — *206*

4　Which two Major League baseball teams play in New York? — *The Yankees and the Mets*

5　Who built the Sphinx? — *The ancient Egyptians*

6　How many Great Lakes are there? — *Five*

7　What is irrigation? — *The supply of water for crops*

8　Who wrote *Twelfth Night*, *Hamlet*, and *Macbeth*? — **William Shakespeare**

9　Han Solo first appeared in which movie? — **Star Wars**

10　Where is the Amazon rain forest? — *In South America (mainly in Brazil)*

Quiz 41
Question 9

Quiz 41
Question 7

Quiz 43 Level 2

Questions	Answers
1 Which island is at the toe of Italy?	*Sicily*
2 Who are the infantry?	*Soldiers who fight on foot*
3 The Chinese were making ice cream some 5,000 years ago. True or false?	*True*
4 Which people wrote in hieroglyphics?	*The ancient Egyptians*
5 Which creature did St. George slay?	*A dragon*
6 What is the capital of Germany?	*Berlin*
7 What is another word for *unite*?	*Join*
8 Is alcohol a drug?	*Yes*
9 What is a cylinder?	*It is a tube shaped like a tin can*
10 What is kelp?	*Seaweed*

Quiz 44
Question 6

Quiz 44
Question I

Quiz 44 Level 2

Questions   ## Answers

1 ❓ Punch and Judy are what? — *Puppets*

2 ❓ Who lived in Sherwood Forest? — *Robin Hood*

3 🍃 Which animal sprays out a foul-smelling fluid to defend itself? — *The skunk*

4 ❓ Who was the first black president of South Africa? — *Nelson Mandela*

5 ⚛ If I have 36 bananas, how many people can I give 3 to? — *12 people*

6 🍃 Which garden pest is related to the snail? — *The slug*

7 📘 Who was Winnie the Pooh's donkey friend? — *Eeyore*

8 ❓ What is the Indy 500? — *An auto-racing event*

9 ❓ On which coin does Abraham Lincoln appear? — *The cent*

10 ⚛ What happens to your eyes when you sneeze? — *They close*

Quiz 43
Question 5

Quiz 43
Question 3

Quiz 45 Level 2

Questions

Answers

1. Which team sport with a ball and goals is played in a swimming pool?

   Water polo

2. In which country was tea first grown?

   China

   Quiz 46
   Question 5

3. Which is the fastest passenger airplane?

   Supersonic Concorde

4. Which is the wealthiest nation?

   The USA

5. What is the shape of one side of a cube?

   A square

6. Who led Britain through World War II?

   Winston Churchill

7. How often are the Olympic Games held?

   Every 4 years

8. What is another word for *suspend*?

   Hang

9. Which animal is said to have nine lives?

   The cat

10. What is the name for the imaginary line around the middle of the Earth?

    The Equator

Quiz 46
Question 9

Questions

Answers

1	What is the masculine of goose?	*Gander*
2	Which country has a military force called the Foreign Legion?	*France*
3	Which two baseball teams are based in Canadian cities?	*Montreal Expos and Toronto Blue Jays*
4	Which sea does the Nile River flow into?	*The Mediterranean*
5	What is the national emblem of Wales?	*The leek*
6	What is the popular name for the Boeing 747?	*The Jumbo Jet*
7	Why is it dark at night?	*The Earth turns from the Sun*
8	A *Triceratops* was what?	*A dinosaur*
9	What was the bombing of London during World War II called?	*The Blitz*
10	Which is the tallest animal?	*The giraffe*

Quiz 45
Question 6

Quiz 45
Question 9

Quiz 47 Level 2

Questions

Answers

1. What is another word for *difficult*?

   Hard

2. Which forbidden fruit did Adam and Eve eat?

   The apple

3. What is the plural of mother-in-law?

   Mothers-in-law

4. How many sides does an octagon have?

   8

5. Who is the heir apparent to Britain's throne?

   Prince Charles

6. Which plant contains nicotine?

   Tobacco plant

7. Which is the world's biggest animal?

   The blue whale

8. Where would you see lava?

   Pouring from a volcano

Quiz 48
Question 7

9. What was the *Luftwaffe*?

   The German air force

10. What is the Great Barrier Reef in Australia made of?

    Coral

Quiz 48
Question 5

Quiz 48 Level 2

Questions	Answers
1 What do *too many cooks* do?	*Spoil the broth*
2 What are back, breast, and crawl?	*Swimming strokes*
3 What were zeppelins?	*Early German airships*
4 What's behind your ribs?	*Your lungs*
5 Which legendary ancient city is said to have sunk beneath the sea?	*Atlantis*
6 Which country is famous for canals, windmills, and bulb fields?	*Holland*
7 How many sides does a cube have?	*6 square sides*
8 How many people play or sing in a quartet?	*4*
9 What sank the S.S. *Titanic*?	*An iceberg*
10 Where is Mount Fujiyama?	*In Japan*

Quiz 47
Question 2

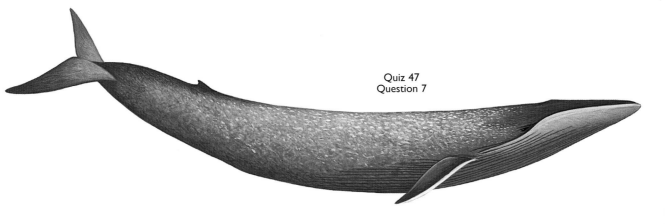

Quiz 47
Question 7

Questions

Answers

		Questions	Answers
1		What is a large ship powered by oars called?	*A galley*
2		Did hussars and dragoons fight on foot or on horse?	*On horse*
3		Which spooky character was created by writer Bram Stoker?	*Dracula*
4		Which Greek conqueror founded the Egyptian city of Alexandria?	*Alexander the Great*
5		Which Asian invaders were led by Attila in 434?	*The Huns*
6		For what did the ancient Egyptians use a *shaduf*: moving stones or raising water?	*Raising water*
7		Which was the last of the single numbers to be invented?	*0 (zero)*
8		Was Mary Cassat a prison reformer or a painter?	*A painter*
9		What was a central marketplace called in ancient Greece?	*The agora*
10		Why did cleaning carpets become simpler after 1876?	*The first carpet sweeper machine was invented*

Quiz 50
Question 3

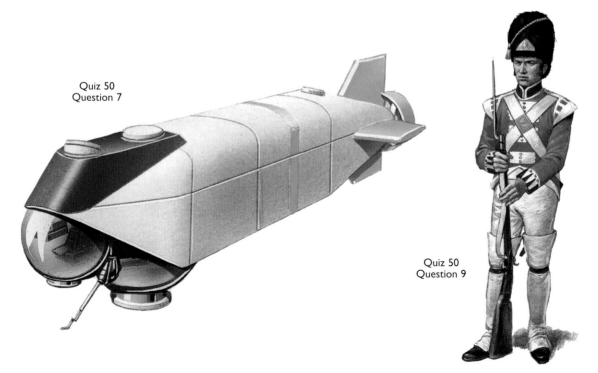

Quiz 50
Question 7

Quiz 50
Question 9

Quiz 50 Level 2

Questions　　　　　　　　　　　　Answers

		Questions	Answers
1		Which English game, invented in the 1700s, uses a bat and ball?	*Cricket*
2	?	What surface was a fresco painted on?	*Fresh plaster*
3	?	Which came first, the Bronze Age or the Iron Age?	*The Bronze Age*
4		Where was the world's first dam built?	*Egypt*
5	?	What were stewponds used for in medieval monasteries?	*Raising fish for food*
6		Why were frogmen so called?	*Because they wore flippers to swim*
7	?	Where might you go in a bathyscaphe?	*Under the sea*
8		By what name was the outlaw William Bonney better known?	*Billy the Kid*
9		Infantrymen and cavalrymen are different types of what?	*Soldier*
10	?	Was Jesse James a real person?	*Yes*

Quiz 49
Question 5

Quiz 49
Question 1

Quiz 51 Level 2

Questions   Answers

1	In which country was the composer Beethoven born?	Germany
2	From which country did the soldiers called hoplites come?	Greece
3	Who was the winged messenger of the Greek gods?	Hermes
4	What was President Lincoln's nickname?	"Honest Abe"
5	What is roughly 4.6 billion years old?	The Earth
6	Where was the Battle of Alamein fought in 1942?	In the North African desert
7	What name did Octavius take when he first became Roman Emperor?	Augustus
8	Ancient Egyptians wrote on a reed called papyrus. What modern word comes from this?	Paper
9	Of which country is Robert Burns the national poet?	Scotland
10	What was the Colosseum in Rome used for?	Gladiator games

Quiz 52
Question 5

Quiz 52
Question 8

Quiz 52 Level 2

Questions

Answers

Quiz 51
Question 4

1. What kind of car set the first world land speed record in 1898? — *An electric car*

2. Was Ted Hughes a poet, a sculptor, or a painter? — *A poet*

3. What kind of animal was Moby Dick? — *A white whale*

4. Which country was the first to use jet planes in war? — *Germany (during World War II)*

5. The Aborigines are the native people of which country? — *Australia*

6. Which sporting event took place for the first time in Greece in 1896? — *The modern Olympics*

7. Did Agatha Christie write funny stories, detective novels, or horror stories? — *Detective novels*

8. Which legendary English king was crowned when he pulled the sword *Excalibur* from the stone? — *King Arthur*

9. Which kind of mill was invented in Iran and came to Europe in about AD1000? — *The windmill*

10. Of what was John McAdam a pioneer? — *Roadbuilding*

Quiz 51
Question 10

Quiz 53 Level 2

Questions   ## Answers

#		Question	Answer
1		What was the Archimedes screw used for?	*Raising water*
2		How many wings does a biplane have?	*Two*
3		Did Leonardo da Vinci ever build a flying machine?	*No: he drew plans for one, but it never flew*
4		In which country was the first bike race held, in 1868?	*France*
5		Who was Baron von Richtofen?	*A German fighter pilot of World War I*
6		In which Anglo-Saxon poem does the monster Grendel appear?	*Beowulf*
7		What did the Minotaur of Greek myths look like?	*It had a man's body and a bull's head*
8		What was a siege tower used for?	*Getting into a castle (over the walls)*
9		In which century were cannons first fired in battle—11th, 14th, or 16th?	*14th century*
10		Is it true that the first eyeglasses were held in the hand?	*Yes*

Quiz 54
Question 6

Quiz 54
Question 9

Quiz 54 Level 2

Questions

Answers

1		Which planet was first seen in 1846?	*Neptune*
2		What was the name of Alexander the Great's favorite horse?	*Bucephalus*
3		Where was the empire ruled by Akbar the Great?	*India*
4		Which famous battle took place in 1916?	*Somme*
5		On which river was Rome built?	*The Tiber*
6		Who was in charge of the British forces at the Battle of Waterloo?	*The Duke of Wellington*
7		Rod Laver became one of Australia's most famous sportsman: in which sport?	*Tennis*
8		Which part of the body was used to measure an inch?	*The first thumb joint*
9		Who built the world's first practical airplane?	*The Wright Brothers*
10		In the Bible, which shepherd boy killed the giant Goliath?	*David*

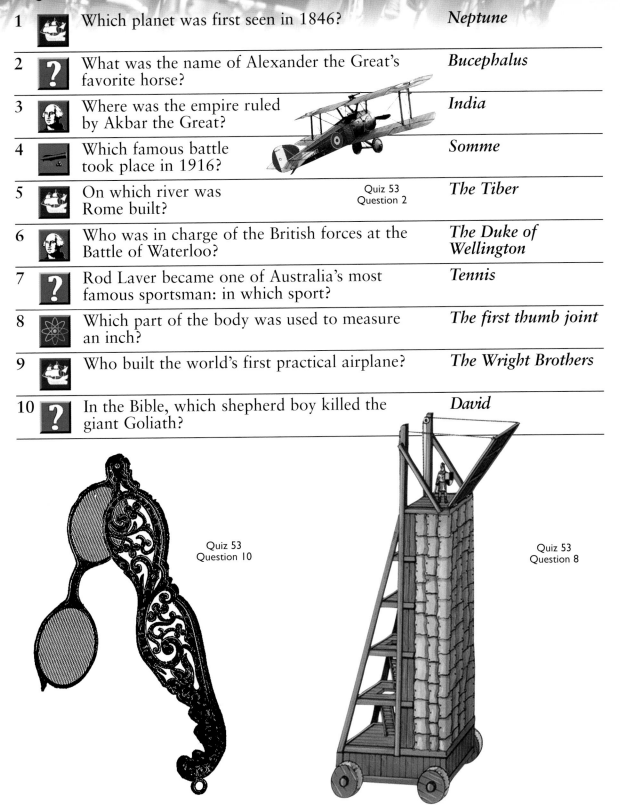

Quiz 53
Question 2

Quiz 53
Question 10

Quiz 53
Question 8

Quiz 55 Level 2

Questions

Answers

		Questions	Answers
1		What did abolitionists campaign to end in the 19th century?	*Slavery*
2		Ulysses is another name for which Greek hero?	*Odysseus*
3		What filled the first balloon to carry passengers?	*Hot air*
4		Which European country has the oldest parliament: Britain, Iceland, or France?	*Iceland*
5		What was the job of the Roman god Mercury?	*Messenger of the gods*
6		What name is given to the ancient Egyptian form of picture writing?	*Hieroglyphs*
7		In which war were Haig and Pershing famous commanders?	*World War I*
8		Which country started the world's first public TV service in 1936?	*Britain*
9		Which president succeeded Franklin Roosevelt in 1945?	*Harry S. Truman*
10		Which type of soldier fought in the Crusades?	*Knights*

Quiz 56
Question 9

Quiz 56 Level 2

Questions

		Questions		Answers
1		Which ocean did Charles Lindbergh fly across in 1927?		*The Atlantic*
2		How long is the Great Wall of China: 300 miles or 3,000 miles?		*3,000 miles*
3		Was Tarzan a real person?		*No*
4		What "out of this world" event happened on July 20, 1969?	Quiz 55 Question 5	*Humans first landed on the Moon*
5		Which Roman poet wrote the long poem called the *Aeneid*?		*Virgil*
6		What was the name of the ancient route which linked China with the West?		*The Silk Road*
7		What were troubadours in the Middle Ages?		*Wandering minstrels (musicians)*
8		Which Italian city has a famous leaning tower, completed in the 1360s?		*Pisa*
9		How long ago did the first farmers live?		*About 10,000 years ago*
10		In which year did the Romans successfully invade Britain?		AD*43*

Quiz 55
Question 10

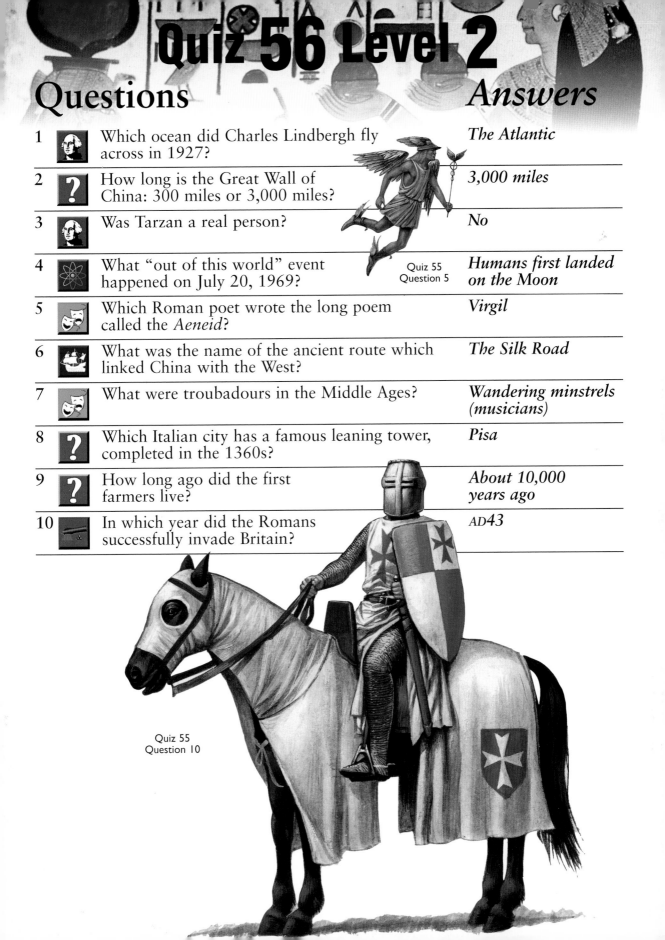

Quiz 57 Level 2

Questions

Answers

Quiz 58
Question 8

		Questions	Answers
1	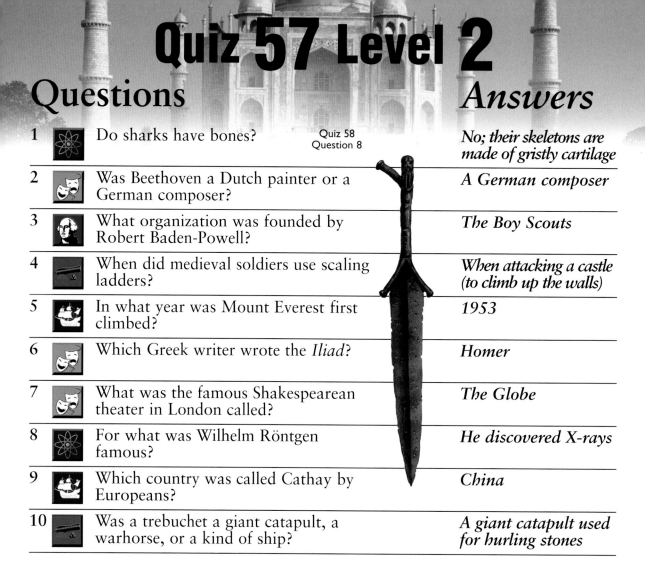	Do sharks have bones?	No; their skeletons are made of gristly cartilage
2		Was Beethoven a Dutch painter or a German composer?	A German composer
3		What organization was founded by Robert Baden-Powell?	The Boy Scouts
4		When did medieval soldiers use scaling ladders?	When attacking a castle (to climb up the walls)
5		In what year was Mount Everest first climbed?	1953
6		Which Greek writer wrote the *Iliad*?	Homer
7		What was the famous Shakespearean theater in London called?	The Globe
8		For what was Wilhelm Röntgen famous?	He discovered X-rays
9		Which country was called Cathay by Europeans?	China
10		Was a trebuchet a giant catapult, a warhorse, or a kind of ship?	A giant catapult used for hurling stones

Quiz 58
Question 1

Quiz 58 Level 2

Questions

Answers

		Question	Answer
1		Which castle in London was built at around the time of William the Conqueror?	*The Tower of London*
2		Who is the patron saint of Ireland?	*St. Patrick*
3		Who discovered Botany Bay?	*Captain Cook*
4		Which king was killed at the Battle of Hastings?	*King Harold*
5		What kind of weapon was a ballista?	*An ancient missile launcher*
6		Which English writer wrote *The Canterbury Tales*, about pilgrims on their way to Canterbury?	*Chaucer*
7		Which white marble mausoleum at Agra, India, took 20,000 men over 20 years to complete?	*Taj Mahal*
8		About when did the Iron Age begin: 19,000BC, 1900BC, or 190BC?	*1900BC*
9		What was the Kon-Tiki which crossed the Pacific: a raft, a balloon, or a canoe?	*A raft*
10		Which European people sailed in longships?	*The Vikings*

Quiz 57
Question 6

Quiz 57
Question 7

Quiz 59 Level 2

Questions

Answers

		Questions	Answers
1		Who painted the *Mona Lisa*?	*Leonardo da Vinci*
2		Was the Mustang a famous fighter plane or a kind of gun?	*A U.S. fighter plane, used in World War II*
3		Who traveled nonstop around the world in a balloon in 1999?	*Brian James and Bertrand Picard*
4		Who created the Church of England to divorce his first wife?	*King Henry VIII*
5		Who in the Bible lost his strength when his hair was cut?	*Samson*
6		Which famous explorer was killed in Hawaii in 1779?	*Captain Cook*
7		What was the first antibiotic drug?	*Penicillin*
8		In which country is a warrior called El Cid a national hero?	*Spain*
9		Which of the Seven Wonders of the Ancient World was in the city of Babylon?	*The Hanging Gardens*
10		Who wrote *Moby Dick*?	*Herman Melville*

Quiz 60
Question 4

Quiz 60
Question 2

Quiz 60
Question 8

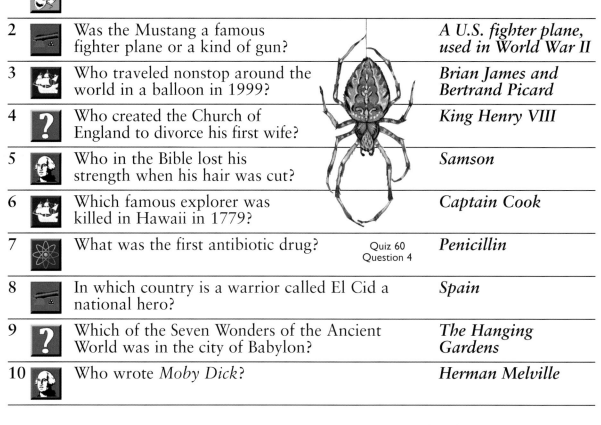

Quiz 60 Level 2

Questions

Answers

		Questions	Answers
1		At which battle did Native American Indians defeat General Custer?	*Battle of the Little Big Horn*
2		Giuseppe Garibaldi is a famous soldier in which European country?	*Italy*
3		To where did a Viking named Leif Ericsson sail?	*North America*
4		Which animal inspired King Robert the Bruce of Scotland to try again?	*A spider*
5		Which tramp with a derby hat and cane was much loved in his silent movies?	*Charlie Chaplin*
6		What animal gave milk to the twins Romulus and Remus when they were left to die?	*A she-wolf*
7		Which naturalist sailed around the world in *The Beagle*?	*Charles Darwin*
8		For what occupation was Jesus trained?	*Carpentry*
9		In which war was the Battle of the Somme?	*World War I (1914-1918)*
10		Did Sir Francis Chichester sail around the world or fly the Pacific in a balloon?	*He sailed around the world, in 1967*

BRITISH ANTARCTIC TERRITO

Republic of Maldives

CAPT. JAMES COOK
250th
ANNIVERSARY
OF BIRTH

1/2p   1L

Quiz 59
Question 6

Quiz 59
Question 4

Quiz 61 Level 2

Questions   Answers

1	What is 68 x 10?	*680*
2	Which force pulls everything to the ground?	*Gravity*
3	What is 16 x 5?	*80*
4	What kind of boat can carry cars, trucks, and trains across water?	*A ferry*
5	What is the difference between a planet and a star?	*A planet has no heat and light of its own*
6	After the Sun, what is the brightest object in the sky?	*The Moon*
7	What instrument would an astronomer use to look at the stars?	*A telescope*
8	What grows to protect the tips of your fingers and toes?	*Your nails*
9	Do climbing boots have rough or smooth soles?	*Rough*
10	What is 3/4 of 100?	*75*

Quiz 62
Question 10

Quiz 62
Question 2

Quiz 62 Level 2

Questions

Answers

1	$\sqrt{x}$	What is 1/4 + 1/4?	*1/2*
2		Your skeleton is made up of 206 what?	*Bones*
3	$\sqrt{x}$	What is the difference between 36 and 60?	*24*
4		What was a penny farthing?	*A bicycle*
5		Which hot drinks contain caffeine?	*Coffee and tea*
6		What part of your body has a sole?	*Your foot*
7		What material is made from animal skins?	*Leather*
8	$\sqrt{x}$	3D shapes can be measured three ways: how long, how wide, and how what?	*High*
9		What shape does a full moon make in the night sky?	*A circle*
10		Is a cello a stringed or a wind instrument?	*Stringed*

Quiz 61
Question 8

Quiz 61
Question 4

Quiz 63 Level 2

Questions   Answers

1 How many grams in half a kilogram?   *500*

2 What is the name of our galaxy?   *The Milky Way*

3 What part of your body does   *Your brain*
   your skull protect?

4 What is a laboratory?   Quiz 64 Question 3   *A room where scientists work*

5 Which organ pumps blood around your body?   *Your heart*

6 What fills with hot water to heat a room?   *A radiator*

7 What are the roof and walls of a greenhouse *Glass*
   usually made of?

8 In 1783, what kind of aircraft carried the first air *A balloon*
   passengers?

9 How much of a circle is a semicircle?   *Half*

10 What is another name for a whirlwind?   *A tornado*

Quiz 64
Question 9

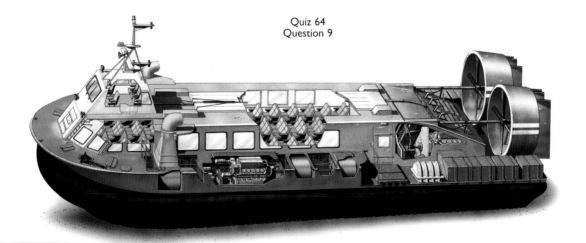

Quiz 64 Level 2

Questions   ## Answers

#	Question	Answer
1	In Roman numerals, what is the symbol for zero?	*There is no symbol for zero*
2	Why does an astronaut need to carry oxygen?	*Because there is no air in space*
3	What is the joint that lets you bend your leg?	*Knee*
4	What does an architect design?	*Buildings*
5	What sounds louder, a noise made near or far away?	*A noise made near*
6	Which instrument do we use to measure weight?	*Scales*
7	What holds a broken bone in place while it mends?	*A plaster cast*
8	Which of these materials is waterproof: wool, plastic, or cotton?	*Plastic*
9	What kind of boat floats along on air?	*A hovercraft*
10	What fraction of a cake does each person get if it is divided between 8 people?	*1/8*

Quiz 63
Question 8

Quiz 63
Question 6

Quiz 65 Level 2

Questions

Answers

		Questions	Answers
1		Which of your five senses do you use to feel a cat's fur?	*Touch*
2		When the Earth shakes violently what is taking place?	*An earthquake*
3	$\sqrt{x}$	How many tens in 4260?	*426*
4		What is stronger: a thread of silk or a thread of steel?	*A thread of silk*
5	$\sqrt{x}$	How many days are there in five weeks?	*35*
6		What is the name for the black and white stripes printed on most of the things we buy?	*The barcode*
7		How many planets are there in the solar system?	*Nine*
8		What is the joint that lets you bend your arm?	*Elbow*
9		What are bubbles full of?	*Air*
10	$\sqrt{x}$	What fraction do you need to add to 5/8 to make a whole?	*3/8*

Quiz 66
Question 4

Quiz 66
Question 6

Quiz 66 Level 2

Questions   ## Answers

1		What supports a building?	*The foundations*
2		What is a shooting star?	*A piece of burning space dust*
3	$\sqrt{x}$	How many degrees is a whole turn?	*360*
4		What pull your bones and let you move?	*Muscles*
5		Does stainless steel rust?	*No*
6		What is the layer of air around Earth called?	*The atmosphere*
7	$\sqrt{x}$	If you opened out a cylinder, what shape would it be?	*A rectangle*
8		What are the five senses?	*Sight, hearing, touch, smell, and taste*
9		What was Stephenson's *Rocket*?	*A steam train*
10	$\sqrt{x}$	What does an inventor do?	*Makes something for the first time*

Quiz 65
Question 8

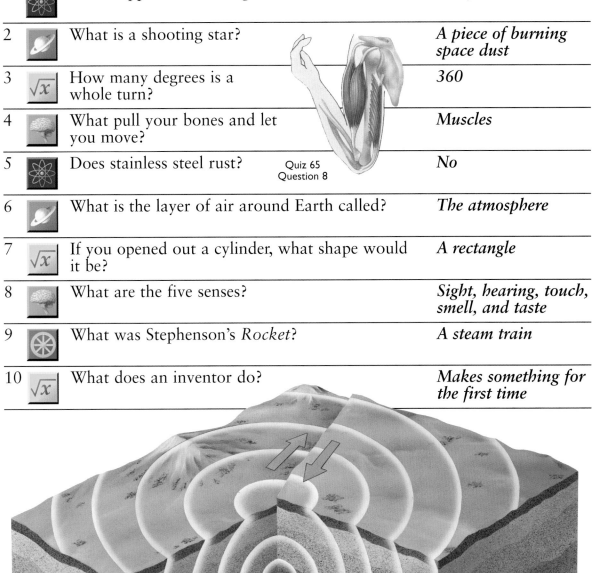

Quiz 65
Question 2

Quiz 67 Level 2

Questions   ## Answers

1	Rubies, diamonds, and emeralds are examples of what?	*Precious stones*
2	How many decimeters in a meter?	*10*
3	Which planet is nearest the Sun?	*Mercury*
4	What is the name for the imaginary line around the middle of the Earth?	*The Equator*
5	Where would you find your calf muscle?	*In your leg*
6	Which number divided by six gives six?	*36*
7	What is carried around your body in veins and arteries?	*Blood*
8	What is special about a bicycle called a tandem?	*It carries two riders*
9	Does oil mix with water?	*No*
10	How many meters in a kilometer?	*1,000*

Quiz 68
Question 5

Quiz 68
Question 6

Quiz 68 Level 2

Questions   ## Answers

1	What has sails that turn around in the wind to work machinery?	*A windmill*
2	How many degrees is half a turn?	*180*
3	What is another name for an elevator?	*A lift*
4	A year on Mercury is only 88 days long. True or false?	*True*
5	What gives your body energy?	*Food*
6	Which animals produce silk?	*Silkworms*
7	What do you find out when you take your temperature?	*How hot you are*
8	What does a zoologist study?	*Animals*
9	Which precious stone is green?	*An emerald*
10	Does a triangle have any parallel sides?	*No*

Quiz 67
Question 1

Quiz 67
Question 8

Quiz 69 Level 2

Questions

Answers

		Question	Answer
1		What happens to water at 100°C?	*It boils*
2	$\sqrt{x}$	If today is Wednesday, what is the day after tomorrow?	*Friday*
3		Which is the odd one out—a stethoscope, a thermometer, a magnet, a hammer?	*A magnet is not a doctor's tool*
4		The Sun moves around the Earth. True or false?	*False, Earth moves around the Sun*
5		Which season brings the coldest weather?	*Winter*
6		What takes place in an operating theater?	*Operations*
7	$\sqrt{x}$	What is the total of 1, 2, 3, 4 and 5?	*15*
8		If something is in motion, what is it doing?	*Moving*
9	$\sqrt{x}$	What is a vertical line on a piece of paper?	*A straight line from top to bottom*
10		Which digging machine has a big blade and moves along on crawler tracks?	*A bulldozer*

Quiz 70
Question 7

Quiz 70
Question 9

Quiz 70 Level 2

Questions

Answers

1	$\sqrt{x}$	How many minutes in a quarter of an hour?	15
2		Where does rubber come from?	Rubber trees
3		Where does a subway train travel?	Underground
4		What is an avalanche?	A fall of snow down a mountainside
5		What is formed when water is surrounded by land?	A lake
6		What is a newborn baby's main food?	Milk
7		Which will feel hotter after stirring a hot drink, a plastic or metal spoon?	A metal spoon
8	$\sqrt{x}$	How much longer is 1 1/2 meters than 75 cms?	75 cms
9		An object staying on the surface of water is doing what?	Floating
10	$\sqrt{x}$	What is the smallest number divisible by both 3 and 4?	12

Quiz 69
Question 4

Quiz 69
Question 10

Quiz 71 Level 2

Questions

Answers

1		What is the total of four 2s and two 4s?	16
2		What part of your body has a drum?	*Your ear*
3		What is the name of a little boat that tows a big ship into harbor?	*A tugboat*
4		What provides the energy for a solar powered car?	*The Sun*
5		What would you find in the middle of the Earth?	*Molten rock*
6		What is the largest kind of ship?	*An oil tanker*
7		What fills with air when you breathe in?	*Your lungs*
8		What is the center of an atom called?	*The nucleus*
9		What is the next number in this sequence—30, 27, 24, 21?	*18*
10		Is cotton a natural or made material?	*Natural*

Quiz 72
Question 9

Quiz 72
Question 4

Quiz 72 Level 2

Questions

Answers

		Questions	Answers
1		Iron, steel, and copper are examples of what?	*Metal*
2		Who of these does not work in a hospital— pediatrician, nurse, attorney, surgeon?	*Attorney*
3		A magnet has an East and West pole, true or false?	*False—it has a North and South pole*
4		What is the name for three babies born at the same time?	*Triplets*
5		What happens to water at 0°C?	*It freezes*
6		What is the name for the strip where an aircraft lands?	*A runway*
7		Which times table are these numbers part of— 14, 28, 49, 56?	*7*
8		What happens to paper and wood when they become very hot?	*They catch fire*
9		How many legs do six spiders have?	*48*
10		What travels faster, light or sound?	*Light*

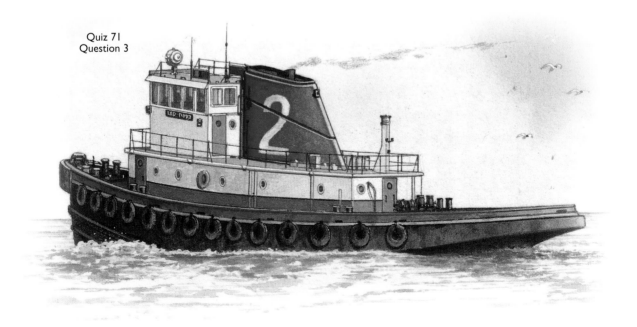

Quiz 71
Question 3

Quiz 73 Level 3

Questions		Answers
1	Which U.S. President was assassinated in Dallas, Texas?	*John F. Kennedy*
2	What is the usual number of kidneys humans have?	*2*
3	What is the main language spoken in Turkey?	*Turkish*
4	What are *Sleeping Beauty*, *Giselle*, and *Swan Lake*?	*Ballets*
5	How many dimes make a dollar?	*Ten*
6	Where is the pupil in your eye?	*In the center of the colored part*
7	*Tyrannosaurus* was what?	*A flesh-eating dinosaur*
8	Where did gladiators originally come from?	*Ancient Rome*
9	What is *to pull the wool over someone's eyes*?	*To deceive someone*
10	Which is the most common infection?	*The common cold*

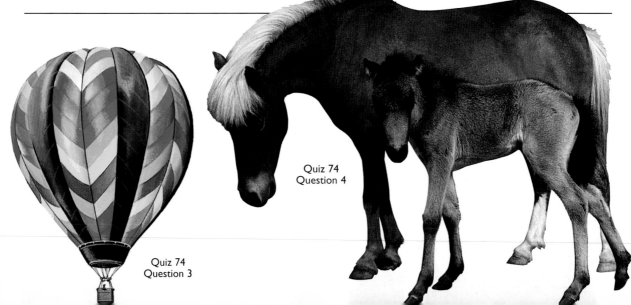

Quiz 74
Question 4

Quiz 74
Question 3

Quiz 74 Level 3

	Questions	Answers
1	What couldn't Jack Sprat eat?	*Fat*
2	Lacrosse was invented in which country?	*Canada*
3	When does an air balloon rise?	*When the air inside it is heated*
4	Where is the mane of a horse?	*Down the back of its neck*
5	Why do some people *knock on wood*?	*To prevent bad luck*
6	Where would you be likely to meet a Maori?	*New Zealand*
7	Cream, butter, cheese, and yogurt are all made from what?	*Milk*
8	Which city are Romulus and Remus supposed to have founded?	*Rome*
9	What is a half of a half?	*A quarter*
10	What makes up a galaxy?	*Stars*

Quiz 73
Question 1

Quiz 73
Question 8

Quiz 75 Level 3

Questions

Answers

		Questions	Answers
1		What is the Italian currency?	*The lira*
2	?	What are judo, karate, kendo, aikado, and kung-fu examples of?	*Martial arts*
3		Where is it dark all day in winter?	*At the North and South Poles*
4		Which animal does ham and pork come from?	*The pig*
5		Children have faster pulse rates than adults. True or false?	*True*
6	?	Who was messenger for the Roman gods?	*Mercury*
7		Which country did Joseph Stalin rule?	*The Soviet Union (Russia)*
8		What do we mean when we say *The pot is calling the kettle black*?	*Criticizing others for your faults*
9		How many straight edges does a cube have?	*12*
10		The Union and Confederate states fought in which war?	*The Civil War*

Quiz 76
Question 4

Quiz 76
Question 7

Quiz 76 Level 3

	Questions	Answers
1	If you read 12 pages a day, how long will it take to read a 60-page book?	*5 days*
2	If the date is 1820, is it the 17th, 18th, or 19th century?	*19th century*
3	What is the currency of Mexico?	*The peso*
4	What do the British call an avocado?	*An avocado pear*
5	What are Labradors, Airedales, and St. Bernards?	*Breeds of dog*
6	Where are Notre Dame, Sacré Cœur, and the Eiffel Tower?	*In Paris*
7	What is the young of a goat called?	*A kid*
8	Who was President before Bill Clinton?	*George Bush*
9	Do you breathe in and out 5 times, 10 times, or 20 times each minute?	*About 20 times when you're resting*
10	Which is the first book of the Bible?	*Genesis*

Quiz 75
Question 6

Quiz 75
Question 4

Quiz 77 Level 3

Questions

Answers

		Questions	Answers
1		A river flows toward the sea. True or false?	*True*
2		How many grams are there in a kilogram?	*1,000*
3		What kind of fruit is used to make wine?	*Grapes*
4		What did the dish run away with?	*The spoon*
5		Which Indian leader led his country in peaceful resistance?	*Mahatma Gandhi*
6		On a compass, which direction is 90 degrees counterclockwise of East?	*North*
7		If a king abdicates, what does he do?	*He gives up his throne*
8		Napoleon Bonaparte was a leader of which country?	*France*
9		Which sea lies between Africa and Europe?	*The Mediterranean*
10		What is lightning?	*An electrical discharge*

Quiz 78
Question 4

Quiz 78
Question 1

Quiz 78 Level 3

Questions

Answers

		Questions	Answers
1		Which flying machine has a rotor and a propeller?	*A helicopter*
2		How can you tell if a shape is symmetrical?	*One fold gives 2 identical halves*
3		Which is the odd one out: Asia, Australia, China, North America?	*China (the others are continents)*
4		Which Australian marsupial looks like a bear?	*The koala*
5		What is the plural of *knife*?	*Knives*
6		How many letters are there in the alphabet?	*26*
7		What is a young deer called?	*A fawn*
8		Where was William the Conqueror from?	*Normandy in France*
9		In which country would you find the towns of Nice and Marseilles?	*France*
10		Which of these numbers are exactly divisible by 3: 6, 8, 12, 24?	*6, 12, 24*

Quiz 77
Question 5

Quiz 77
Question 6

Quiz 77
Question 4

Quiz 79 Level 3

Questions

Answers

1. What work did the Seven Dwarfs do? — *They worked in a mine*

2. What is mutton? — *Meat from sheep over one year old*

3. Where is Bombay? — *India*

4. A spider has how many legs? — *Eight*

5. What emerged from Aladdin's lamp? — *A genie*

6. What are cirrus and cumulus examples of? — *Clouds*

7. What is chocolate made from? — *Cocoa beans*

8. What does temperature measure? — *Heat*

9. The Pony Express carried what through the Wild West? — *Mail*

10. How many meters are there in half a kilometer? — *500*

Quiz 80
Question 5

Quiz 80
Question 4

Quiz 80 Level 3

Questions	Answers
1 What does Popeye eat for strength?	Spinach
2 Which part of an airplane is the fuselage?	The body
3 How many blackbirds were baked in the pie?	24
4 Which limbs of the *Venus de Milo* are missing?	The arms
5 Which animal is usually ridden in the desert?	The camel
6 Can you ride on African elephants?	No, only on Indian elephants
7 Which of these numbers can be divided by both 3 and 4: 9, 12, 15, 16?	12
8 In which English city was there a great fire in 1666?	London
9 A recipe needs 7 ounces of milk, I have $2^1/_2$ ounces. How much do I need?	$4^1/_2$ ounces
10 With which color is Robin Hood associated?	Green

Quiz 79
Question 3

Quiz 79
Question 5

Quiz 81 Level 3

Questions	Answers
1 How many points does a field goal score in football?	3
2 How many fiddlers did Old King Cole have?	3
3 Who wore a coat of many colors?	*Joseph*
4 Iceberg and Boston are types of what?	*Lettuce*
5 Where is the bow of a ship?	*At the front*
6 Which bird lays the largest egg?	*The ostrich*
7 Which is larger: 8 x 14 or 14 x 8?	*Neither. They both equal 112*
8 What did Guy Fawkes try to blow up?	*The Houses of Parliament*
9 What are Catherine wheels and Roman candles examples of?	*Fireworks*
10 Where is Venice?	*Italy*

Quiz 82
Question 7

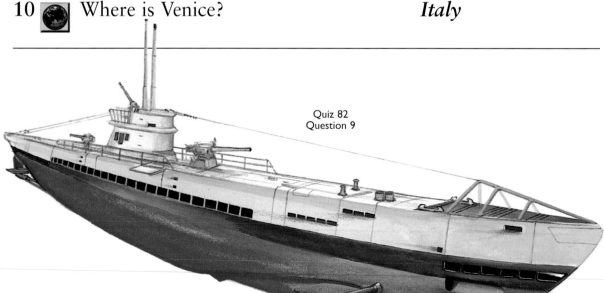

Quiz 82
Question 9

Quiz 82 Level 3

Questions

Answers

		Question	Answer
1		What is the opposite of the word *brave*?	*Cowardly*
2		The date is May 10th. What will the date be in two weeks' time?	*May 24th*
3	?	What does a confectioner sell?	*Candy and other sweets*
4		What is a quarter of a half?	*An eighth*
5		Which U.S. state is made up completely of islands?	*Hawaii*
6		What is the plural of sheep?	*Sheep*
7		Frog spawn, tadpole. What comes next?	*Frog*
8		What is the name for a moving staircase?	*An escalator*
9		What were German submarines called?	*U-boats*
10	?	For which sport would you practice on nursery slopes?	*Skiing*

Quiz 81
Question 4

Quiz 81
Question 10

Quiz 83 Level 3

	Questions	Answers
1	Does air have weight?	Yes
2	What is the capital of the United Kingdom?	London
3	Which queen ruled Britain for 64 years?	Queen Victoria
4	How many 4s are there in 56?	14
5	If today is Tuesday, what was the day before yesterday?	Sunday
6	What word do we use for a book of maps?	An atlas
7	How many meters are there in 4.5 km?	4,500
8	Munich, Berlin, and Hamburg are in which country?	Germany
9	Which of these animals is a carnivore: squirrel, leopard, rabbit, or giraffe?	The leopard
10	What is the opposite of generous?	Stingy

Quiz 84
Question 7

Quiz 84 Level 3

	Questions	Answers
1	In which country are the Prairie provinces?	Canada
2	In which game is a shuttlecock used?	Badminton
3	What is the plural of mouse?	Mice
4	In which century is 1314?	14th
5	Where is Uluru?	Australia
6	What do you call a barrier that holds back water?	A dam
7	Which airplane carries the most passengers?	A Jumbo Jet
8	Where are your incisors?	In your mouth (they are teeth)
9	How many wives did King Henry VIII have?	6
10	What is the past tense of eat?	Ate

Quiz 83
Question 9

Quiz 83
Question 3

Quiz 85 Level 3

Questions

Answers

1. **?** What is the national currency of France?

   The franc

2. What tree does an acorn come from?

   The oak

3. What are forget-me-nots and marigolds examples of?

   Flowers

4. What is another name for a microprocessor in a computer?

   A microchip or a silicon chip

5. What is 7 less than 3,000?

   2,993

6. **?** What is an ingot?

   A brick-shaped bar of metal

   Quiz 85
   Question 3

7. What did the dinosaur *Stegosaurus* have on its back?

   Large, upright plates

8. Which games, held every 4 years, first took place in ancient Greece?

   The Olympic Games

9. **?** What are wing tips, loafers, and brogues?

   Types of shoe

10. Handel, Mozart, and Brahms were all what?

    Composers

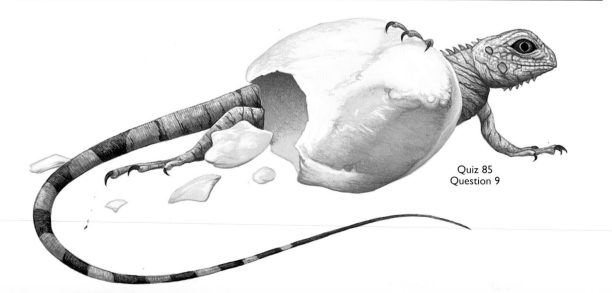

Quiz 85
Question 9

Quiz 86 Level 3

Questions	Answers

Questions

Answers

1. The United States bought Louisiana from which European country? — *France*

2. What has the head and body of a woman and a long fish tail? — *A mermaid, according to legend*

3. The tubing of which brass wind instrument is curved into circles? — *The French horn*

4. In a desert, what is an area that has water called? — *An oasis*

5. What is an igloo made from? — *Blocks of snow and ice*

6. What shape is the base of a pyramid? — *A square*

7. Which country has the largest population? — *China*

8. In which sport are there lets, lobs, and aces? — *Tennis*

9. Is an iguana—a bird, marsupial or reptile? — *A reptile*

10. What is a group of elephants called? — *A herd*

Quiz 86
Question 3

Quiz 86
Question 7

Quiz 87 Level 3

Questions

Answers

		Questions	Answers
1	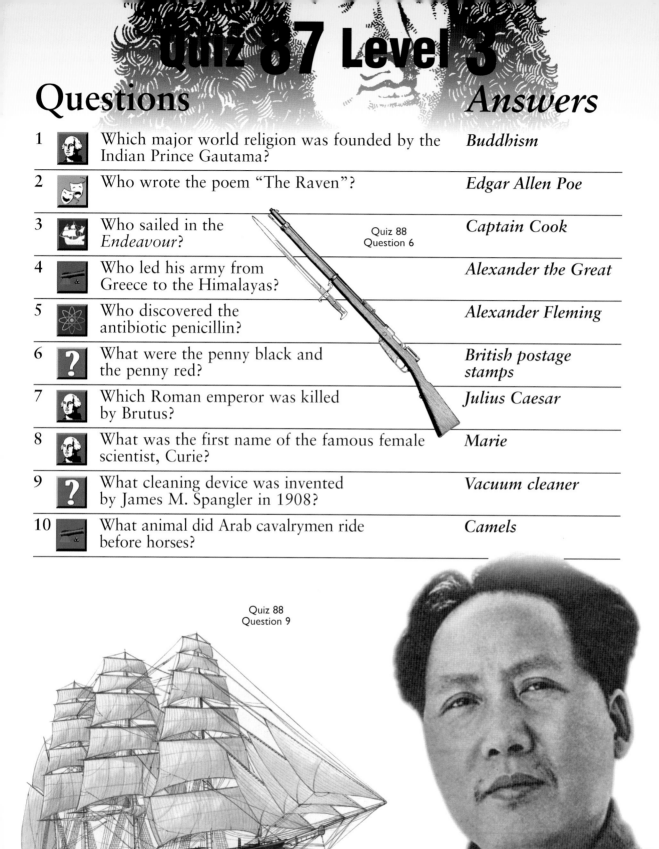	Which major world religion was founded by the Indian Prince Gautama?	*Buddhism*
2		Who wrote the poem "The Raven"?	*Edgar Allen Poe*
3		Who sailed in the *Endeavour*?	*Captain Cook*
4		Who led his army from Greece to the Himalayas?	*Alexander the Great*
5		Who discovered the antibiotic penicillin?	*Alexander Fleming*
6		What were the penny black and the penny red?	*British postage stamps*
7		Which Roman emperor was killed by Brutus?	*Julius Caesar*
8		What was the first name of the famous female scientist, Curie?	*Marie*
9		What cleaning device was invented by James M. Spangler in 1908?	*Vacuum cleaner*
10		What animal did Arab cavalrymen ride before horses?	*Camels*

Quiz 88
Question 6

Quiz 88
Question 9

Quiz 88
Question 5

Quiz 88 Level 3

Questions   ## Answers

1	Which volcano covered the Italian town of Pompeii with ash in AD62?	Vesuvius
2	Which coast did Matthew Flinders explore in about 1800?	Australian
3	Which French king built the Palace of Versailles?	Louis XIV (the Fourteenth)
4	Which Irish saint was once captured and sold as a slave?	Patrick
5	Who led the Communist Revolution in China?	Mao Tse-tung (Mao Zedong)
6	Where did a soldier fix a bayonet?	On the end of his rifle
7	Which continent is named after Amerigo Vespucci (1454-1512)?	America
8	Which country used to have an emperor called the kaiser?	Germany
9	What were "clipper" ships famous for carrying?	Tea
10	Which god in Hindu mythology has an elephant's head?	Ganesh

Quiz 87
Question 9

Quiz 87
Question 10

Quiz 87
Question 7

Quiz 89 Level 3

Questions   Answers

		Questions	Answers
1		Who wrote *Treasure Island*?	*Robert Louis Stevenson*
2		Was Lizzie Borden a famous murderer or the inventor of Mickey Mouse?	*A famous murderer*
3		Who was nicknamed the "Lady of the Lamp" during the Crimean war?	*Florence Nightingale*
4		How many of Magellan's ships sailed home after circling the world in 1522?	*One*
5		What was the first mass-produced car in 1908?	*The Ford Model-T*
6		What changed the way books were made in the 1400s?	*The invention of printing with movable type*
7		How many children has Queen Elizabeth II of Britain?	*Four*
8		Which country had the first roadside gas pump?	*The USA (in 1906)*
9		Which Russian composer wrote the *1812 Overture*?	*Tchaikovsky*
10		To which country did Marco Polo journey?	*China*

Quiz 90
Question 3

Quiz 90
Question 8

Quiz 90 Level 3

Questions

Answers

#		Question	Answer
1		Did the first bicycles have pedals?	No, *they were were pushed along*
2		In which country were Europe's first banks?	*Italy*
3		What was the system called under which serfs worked for the lord?	*The feudal system*
4		Who tried to blow up the British Houses of Parliament in 1605?	*Guy Fawkes*
5		What kind of craft was a zeppelin?	*An airship*
6		Who invented the lightning rod?	*Benjamin Franklin*
7		Which state is named for Queen Elizabeth I of England?	*Virginia (for the "Virgin Queeen")*
8		Hoplite soldiers from which country fought in a phalanx?	*Greece*
9		How long was the pike used by Alexander the Great's soldiers: 3 feet, 10 feet, or 20 feet?	*20 feet*
10		Was Leonardo da Vinci born near Florence, Italy, or in Vienna, Austria?	*Near Florence, Italy*

Quiz 89
Question 8

Quiz 89
Question 3

Quiz 89
Question 5

Quiz 91 Level 3

Questions   ## Answers

1		Which people invented the magnetic compass?	*The Chinese*
2		Which holy book was first written down by the prophet Muhammad?	*The Koran*
3		Which country attacked Pearl Harbor in 1941?	*Japan*
4		Which explorer, who discovered America, sailed in the *Santa Maria*?	*Christopher Columbus*
5		In which Greek city is the Parthenon?	*Athens*
6		What fell on Newton's head, according to one story?	*An apple (making him think about gravity)*
7		In which war were V-1 flying bombs used?	*World War II (1939-1945)*
8		Which great river flowed through ancient Egypt?	*The Nile*
9		What device helped the Greeks to capture the city of Troy?	*A wooden horse*
10		In which century did the Industrial Revolution begin?	*18th (1700s)*

Quiz 92
Question 10

Quiz 92
Question 2

Quiz 92
Question 8

Quiz 92 Level 3

Questions | Answers

		Questions	Answers
1		Which two countries began a "space race" in 1957?	*USSR and the United States*
2	**?**	Who laid down his cloak to keep Queen Elizabeth I's feet dry?	*Sir Walter Raleigh*
3		When were X-rays discovered?	*1895*
4		Which Johnson was a famous aviator: Amy, Jack, or Lyndon?	*Amy Johnson*
5		Who was the Norse god of thunder?	*Thor*
6		Which Roman emperor ordered the building of a frontier wall across northern England in AD122?	*Hadrian*
7		Which great French scientist made the first vaccine against rabies?	*Louis Pasteur*
8	**?**	What is a blunderbuss?	*A old type of gun*
9		During the Ice Age sea levels dropped. How did this help the first people to reach America?	*They crossed from Asia on exposed land*
10	**?**	In which country is the kimono a form of national dress?	*Japan*

Quiz 91
Question 9

Quiz 91
Question 4

Quiz 93 Level 3

Questions

Answers

1. Which mountain range did Hannibal famously cross with his army and their elephants?

   The Alps

2. Which sea captain sailed in the *Golden Hind*?

   Francis Drake

3. Is the Humboldt current a part of a TV set or water in the ocean?

   It's a cold ocean current off South America

4. Who founded the American state of Pennsylvania?

   William Penn

5. What was a "powder monkey" on an old sailing warship?

   Quiz 94 Question 8

   A boy who carried gunpowder

6. About when did the first modern humans appear: 1,500,000BC, 150,000BC, or 15,000BC?

   150,000BC

7. What kind of farm machine did Cyrus McCormick invent?

   A mechanical harvester

8. Was the Egyptian pharaoh Tutankhamun buried in a pyramid?

   No—he was buried in a tomb

9. In the book *Gulliver's Travels*, are the people from Lilliput large or small?

   Small

10. Who wore bellbottom pants: sailors, soldiers, or airmen?

    Sailors

Quiz 94 Question 2

Quiz 94 Level 3

Questions

Answers

#	Question	Answer
1	Why did early steamships have sails as well as engines?	*In case the engines broke down or ran out of fuel*
2	Of what were the roofs of Bronze Age houses made?	*Thatch (straw)*
3	Who was president of the Confederacy during the U.S. Civil War?	*Jefferson Davis*
4	What name was given to the NASA missions to the Moon?	*Apollo*
5	Who won the battle of Saratoga in 1777?	*The Americans, when the British surrendered*
6	Who wrote the great Greek tragic play *Oedipus Rex*?	*Sophocles*
7	Who commanded HMS *Bounty* on a voyage to the Pacific in 1787?	*Captain William Bligh*
8	Who composed *The Planets* suite between 1914 and 1917?	*Gustav Holst*
9	Who was Frank James's more famous outlaw brother?	*Jesse James*
10	What was the last planet in the solar system to be discovered?	*Pluto, in 1930*

Quiz 93
Question 6

Quiz 93
Question 2

Quiz 93
Question 2

Quiz 95 Level 3

Questions

Answers

1		Why did explorers often carry chickens and goats on board ships?	*For eggs and goats' milk*
2		What is a religious man who lives in a monastery called?	*A monk*
3		Was Amelia Earhart a famous flier, a lone sailor, or a mountaineer?	*A famous flier*
4		What do Henry Irving, Laurence Olivier, and John Gielgud have in common?	*Acting (all three became famous actors)*
5		In the Bible, which unwilling prophet was swallowed by a whale?	*Jonah*
6		Who was a famous American poet in the 1900s: John Milton, Emily Dickinson, or John Keats?	*Emily Dickinson*
7		Which continent did Columbus hope to find by sailing west?	*Asia*
8		Which American playwright wrote *Death of a Salesman*?	*Arthur Miller*
9		For what was Nijinsky famous?	*Ballet dancing*
10		Who discovered the principle of buoyancy in about 250BC?	*Archimedes*

Quiz 96
Question 9

Quiz 96
Question 1

Quiz 96 Level 3

Questions

Quiz 95
Question 2

Answers

#		Question	Answer
1		The people of which ancient "classical" civilization wore togas?	*Rome*
2		Which composer went deaf in his later years?	*Beethoven*
3		When did the ancient Egyptians devise the 365-day calendar?	*2500BC*
4		Did Columbus make just one voyage to the Americas?	*No; he made four*
5		Which country did Napoleon invade in 1812?	*Russia*
6		What day did June 4, 1944 become known as?	*D-Day*
7		What was the nickname of the American Confederate general Thomas Jackson?	*Stonewall*
8		When was gunpowder first used in battle in Europe: 1346, 1446, or 1546?	*1346*
9		Which Scottish king killed King Duncan, but was himself killed by Duncan's son, Malcolm III?	*Macbeth*
10		Who commanded the Southern forces in the U.S. Civil War?	*General Robert E. Lee*

Quiz 95
Question 3

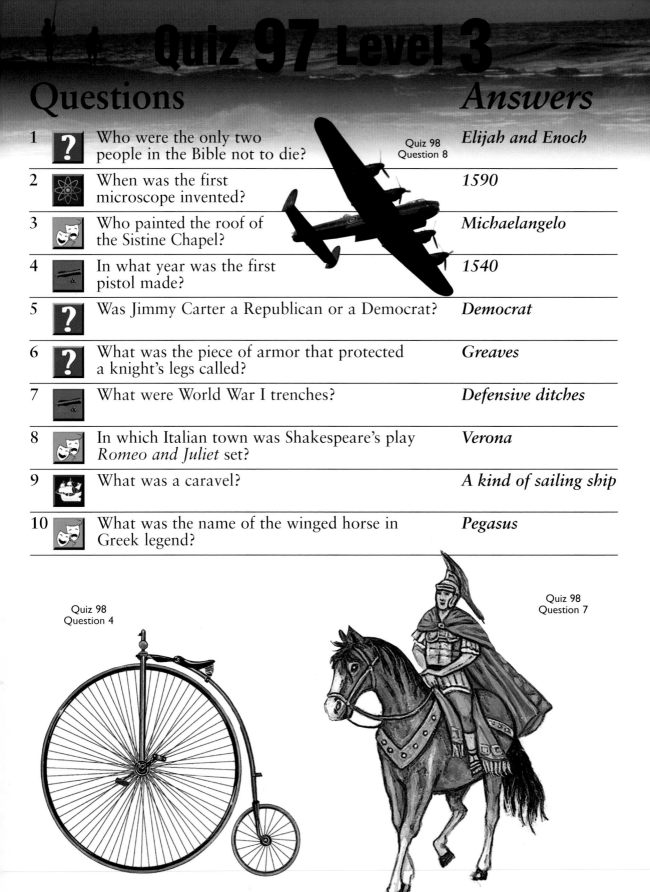

Quiz 97 Level 3

Questions

Answers

		Questions	Answers
1		Who were the only two people in the Bible not to die?	*Elijah and Enoch*
2		When was the first microscope invented?	*1590*
3		Who painted the roof of the Sistine Chapel?	*Michaelangelo*
4		In what year was the first pistol made?	*1540*
5		Was Jimmy Carter a Republican or a Democrat?	*Democrat*
6		What was the piece of armor that protected a knight's legs called?	*Greaves*
7		What were World War I trenches?	*Defensive ditches*
8		In which Italian town was Shakespeare's play *Romeo and Juliet* set?	*Verona*
9		What was a caravel?	*A kind of sailing ship*
10		What was the name of the winged horse in Greek legend?	*Pegasus*

Quiz 98
Question 8

Quiz 98
Question 4

Quiz 98
Question 7

Quiz 98 Level 3

Questions

Answers

		Questions	Answers
1	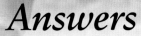	At the tip of which continent is Cape Horn?	*South America*
2		What was a Sopwith Camel in World War I?	*A fighter plane*
3		Who was the first Englishman to sail around the world?	*Sir Walter Raleigh*
4		What was a penny farthing?	*An early bicycle*
5		Was a Tin Lizzie an early car or an early washing machine?	*An early car*
6		In what year was the first steam boat sailed by Claude d'Abbans in France: 1683, 1783, or 1883?	*1783*
7		Did Roman soldiers ride horses?	*Yes*
8		What were Lancasters and Flying Fortresses?	*Bombers used in World War II (1939-1945)*
9		Which ocean did explorers cross to reach India from East Africa?	*The Indian Ocean*
10		Who was the king of the Roman gods?	*Jupiter*

Quiz 97
Question 7

Quiz 99 Level 3

Questions   ## Answers

1	Which queen of England ruled from 1837 to 1901?	Queen Victoria
2	What made sailors suffer from the disease called scurvy?	Not eating fresh fruit and vegetables
3	In 1979, which country was invaded by Soviet troops?	Afghanistan
4	Of which country was Helmut Kohl leader until 1998?	Germany
5	What was the first living creature sent into space in 1957: a dog, a monkey, or a rabbit?	A Russian dog named Laika
6	What is the date for Abraham Lincoln's birthday?	February 12
7	Was Columbus born in Spain or Italy?	Italy
8	Was a pike a long spearlike weapon or a helmet with a spike on top?	A long spearlike weapon
9	In 1642 Abel Tasman landed on a new island that he called Van Diemen's Land. What is it called now?	Tasmania
10	Which Indian leader was known as the Mahatma or "Great Soul"?	Gandhi

Quiz 100
Question 5

Quiz 100
Question 4

Quiz 100 Level 3

Questions   Answers

1	How many actors speak a monologue?	*One*
2	Which German general of World War II was nicknamed The Desert Fox?	*Rommel*
3	This country was once called Siam: what is its modern name?	*Thailand*
4	Explorers in South America caught and ate cavies: what were cavies?	*Guinea pigs*
5	Where did ammonites live: in trees, on the ground, or under the sea?	*Under the sea*
6	What were U-boats?	*German submarines*
7	Who was the first pope?	*The apostle St. Peter*
8	Which country used Zero fighters during World War II?	*Japan*
9	Who is the odd one out of these three leaders: Truman, Macmillan, Bush?	*Macmillan (British PM not U.S. president)*
10	Against whom did Richard the Lionheart fight in the Crusades?	*Saladin*

Quiz 99
Question 7

Quiz 99
Question 8

Quiz 101 Level 3

Questions

Answers

		Questions	Answers
1		What are Sirius, Betelgeuse, and Polaris all examples of?	*Stars*
2	$\sqrt{x}$	Which of these numbers is not exactly divisible by five—10, 12, 30, 45?	*12*
3		Thunder and lightning happen at the same time—true or false?	*True*
4	$\sqrt{x}$	On a compass, which direction is opposite East?	*West*
5		Things become smaller when they are heated—true or false	*False; they become bigger*
6		What did Louis Braille invent in 1837?	*A raised dot alphabet for blind people*
7		What language can you see but not hear?	*Sign language*
8		Is river water fresh or salty?	*Fresh*
9		What is the part of your leg above the knee called?	*Thigh*
10		Does a geologist study stars, rocks, or dinosaurs?	*Rocks*

Quiz 102
Question 6

Quiz 102
Question 2

Quiz 102 Level 3

Questions

Answers

		Questions	Answers
1	$\sqrt{x}$	What shape is the flat base of a cone?	*A circle*
2		What was known as the iron horse when it was first invented?	*A train engine*
3		Does the Sun rise in the East or West?	*In the East*
4		Does your heart beat faster or slower when you run?	*Faster*
5		What color do you get if you mix red and yellow?	*Orange*
6		What is a meteorite?	*A rock from space*
7		If you wave your right hand at a mirror, which hand will your reflection wave back?	*Left*
8		What do you have about five million of growing on your body?	*Hairs*
9		Which of these is not a scientist—physicist, taxidermist, biologist, chemist?	*Taxidermist*
10	$\sqrt{x}$	Which two of these letters have a line of symmetry—A, G, O, F, L?	*A, O*

Quiz 101
Question 6

Quiz 101
Question 7

Quiz 103 Level 3

Questions

Answers

1		When animals and clothes are colored to match surroundings, what is it called?	*Camouflage*
2		What do you see in a planetarium?	*The night sky*
3		Identical twins have the same fingerprints. True or false?	*False*
4		How many sides does a quadrilateral have?	*Four*
5		Where would you find a pupil and an iris?	*In your eye*
6		What color do you get if you mix yellow and blue?	*Green*
7		If the 2nd of February is Wednesday, what day will the 6th of February be?	*Sunday*
8		What kind of work does a machine called an excavator do?	*Digging*
9		How many zeros are there in twenty thousand?	*Four*
10		What is natural history the study of?	*All natural things*

Quiz 104
Question 2

Quiz 104
Question 8

Quiz 104 Level 3

Questions

Answers

		Questions	Answers
1		How many teeth in a full adult set?	32
2		Which planet is well known for its rings?	*Saturn*
3		How many faces does a square-based pyramid have altogether?	*Five*
4		In which season are baby animals usually born?	*Spring*
5		What part of your body has a lobe?	*Your ear*
6		What are the first letters of the seven colors of the rainbow?	*R, O, Y, G, B, I, V*
7		What is the distance between the center and the edge of a circle called?	*The radius*
8		What is the name of a boat that carries cargo along a canal?	*A barge*
9		How many seconds in 1 1/2 minutes?	90
10		What does vibrate mean?	*Move fast to and fro*

Quiz 103
Question 8

Quiz 105 Level 3

Questions

Answers

#		Questions	Answers
1		What are the mixture of gases called that come from a car engine?	*Exhaust*
2		What is a monsoon?	*A very heavy rainstorm*
3		Which kind of triangle has three equal sides?	*An equilateral triangle*
4		Your breathe air in through which two parts of your body?	*Your mouth and nose*
5		What color do you get if you mix red and blue?	*Purple*
6		What are constellations?	*Patterns of stars in the sky*
7		On a 24 hour digital clock, what numbers show at 4 pm?	*16:00*
8		At what times of day can the sky become red?	*Sunrise and sunset*
9		What is the total of five 5s and ten 4s?	*65*
10		The artist Leonardo da Vinci invented a flying machine 500 years ago—true or false?	*True*

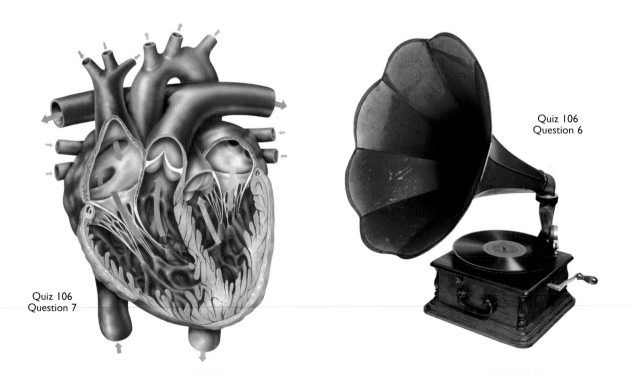

Quiz 106
Question 6

Quiz 106
Question 7

Quiz 106 Level 3

Questions | Answers

#		Question	Answer
1	√x	Which kind of clock measures time by the Sun?	*A sundial*
2		What is another name for perspiration?	*Sweat*
3		What is the name for pieces of ice falling from clouds?	*Hail*
4	√x	Which numbers show on a digital clock at a quarter to 11?	*10:45*
5		What is the band of stars we call the Milky Way?	*The edge of our galaxy*
6		Which invention was first called a phonograph?	*A record player*
7		What part of your body works like a pump?	*Your heart*
8		Which word describes how loud a sound is?	*Volume*
9	√x	How many degrees is half a turn?	*180*
10		What do you do to food to fry it?	*Cook it in hot oil*

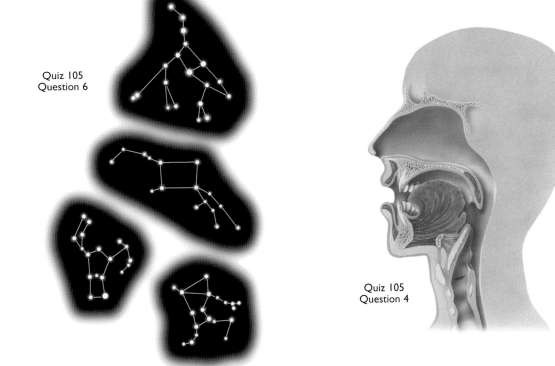

Quiz 105
Question 6

Quiz 105
Question 4

Quiz 107 Level 3

Questions
Answers

#		Question	Answer
1	$\sqrt{x}$	How many right angles does a right-angle triangle have?	*One*
2		Which machine is said to work like an electronic brain?	*A computer*
3		Which is the largest planet in the solar system?	*Jupiter*
4	$\sqrt{x}$	What is 54 divided by 6?	*9*
5		Which of your bones make a cage?	*Ribs*
6		What silver metal is inside a thermometer?	*Mercury*
7		What is the chemical symbol for lead?	*Pb*
8		Which modeling material is made from newspaper, flour, and water?	*Papier-mâché*
9	$\sqrt{x}$	How many minutes long is a program starting at 6:15 and ending at 6:45?	*30*
10		What part of the Earth does a scuba diver explore?	*Under the water*

Quiz 108
Question 10

Quiz 108
Question 4

Quiz 108 Level 3

Questions

Answers

		Questions	Answers
1		When a dentist extracts a tooth, what does she do?	She pulls it out
2		What is the name of a giant wave caused by an earthquake?	A tidal wave
3		What is 3/10 as a decimal?	0.3
4		What is the name for a machine made of ropes and wheels used to lift heavy loads?	A pulley
5		What shape is the Moon a few days after new moon?	A crescent
6		What does your body need eight hours of every day?	Sleep
7		Do you get goose flesh when you are hot or cold?	Cold
8		What is charcoal?	Partly burned wood
9		What is the name for any flat shape with three or more straight sides?	A polygon
10		What makes a car tire grip the road?	The tread pattern

Quiz 107
Question 3

Quiz 109 Level 3

Questions

Answers

		Question	Answer
1		Is plastic a natural or made material?	*Made material*
2		People never stop growing taller. True or false?	*False*
3		In which season do leaves fall from trees?	*Autumn*
4		Which of these numbers can be divided by 5 and 3—9, 20, 27, 30?	*30*
5		What is a hospital room with several beds called?	*A ward*
6		Which planet is farthest away from the Sun?	*Pluto*
7		What does transparent mean?	*See through*
8		Shapes can be 2D or 3D; what does D stand for?	*Dimensions*
9		What is the name for a rod that is used for moving something heavy?	*A lever*
10		Take 20 away from 111	*91*

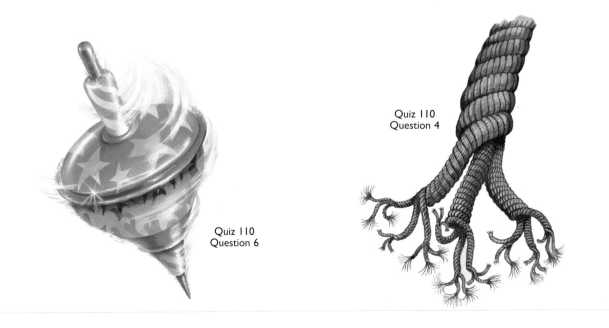

Quiz 110
Question 4

Quiz 110
Question 6

Quiz 110 Level 3

Questions | Answers

#		Question	Answer
1		Natural wool is waterproof. True or false?	*True*
2		Is the North Pole on land or frozen water?	*Frozen water*
3		What appears on your skin when you get a hard knock?	*A bruise*
4		Long fibers twisted together make a strong what?	*Rope*
5		How many legs does a football team have?	*22*
6		When something spins, how does it move?	*Around and around*
7		What do radios and televisions have for picking up signals?	*An antenna*
8		What is the remainder when 48 is divided by 7?	*Six*
9		What part of the body would a dermatologist treat?	*Skin*
10		Where is rain formed?	*In clouds*

Quiz 109
Question 9

Quiz 109
Question 6

Quiz 111 Level 3

Questions

Answers

1		Which does not have a tail: a kite, a boat, or an airplane?	*A boat*
2	$\sqrt{x}$	What instrument is used for drawing circles?	*A compass*
3		Does a meteorologist study meteorites, the ocean, or the weather?	*The weather*
4		Which gas does fire need to burn?	*Oxygen*
5	$\sqrt{x}$	How many seconds in three minutes?	*180*
6		What is used to stop machine parts rubbing together?	*Oil*
7		What part of your body wrinkles when you frown?	*Your forehead*
8		Earth travels through space at 66,500 miles per hour. True or false?	*True*
9		If you had hayfever, what would you be allergic to?	*Pollen*
10	$\sqrt{x}$	Which angle is greater, a 45° angle or a 90° angle?	*A 90° angle*

Quiz 112
Question 3

Quiz 112
Question 1

Quiz 112 Level 3

Questions
Answers

		Question	Answer
1		What has hands, a face, and wheels?	*A clock*
2		What did Clarence Birdseye invent in 1924?	*Frozen food*
3		What is the name of a giant block of ice floating in the sea?	*An iceberg*
4		Why is blinking good for your eyes? Quiz 111 Question 2	*It keeps them clean*
5		What are the two passages in your nose called?	*Nostrils*
6		Do all metals melt when they are hot?	*Yes*
7		When something ignites, what happens to it?	*It catches fire*
8		What is the name for walls of rock that go down to the sea?	*Cliffs*
9		How many times does 8 divide into 72?	*9*
10		What is the total of three 3s and seven 4s?	*37*

Quiz 111
Question 9

Quiz 111
Question 4

Quiz 113 Level 3

Questions
Answers

		Questions	Answers
1		What do vaccinations protect you from?	*Infectious diseases*
2		Does electricity flow through metal or rubber?	*Metal*
3		What makes a jack-in-the-box jump out of its box?	*A spring*
4		Put these numbers in order starting with the smallest—532, 629, 423?	*423, 532, 629*
5		Are the letters on a computer keyboard lower case or upper case?	*Upper case*
6		What do we call the imaginary points at either end of the Earth?	*North and South Poles*
7		Which end of binoculars do you look through to make things look farther away?	*The wide end*
8		In which continent would you find zebras and elephants?	*Africa*
9		What is 0.25 as a fraction?	*1/4*
10		Is sound a form of energy?	*Yes*

Quiz 114
Question 1

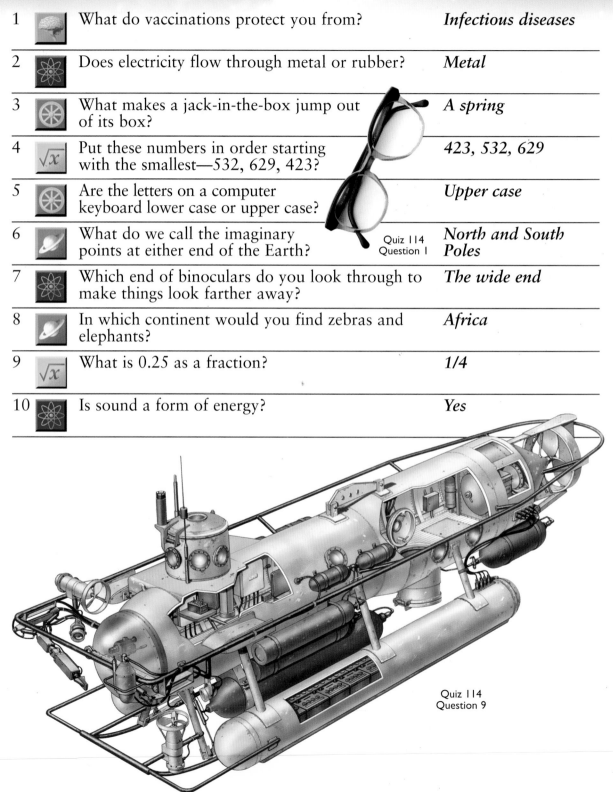

Quiz 114
Question 9

Quiz 114 Level 3

	Questions	Answers
1	What is the curved glass in a telescope called?	*A lens*
2	What black powder did the Chinese invent to make fireworks?	*Gunpowder*
3	What is 50% of 80?	*40*
4	What material stretches when it is pulled?	*Elastic*
5	Which number is not exactly divisible by 7—7, 17, 21, 14, 28?	*17*
6	What would you lose if you had laryngitis?	*Your voice*
7	What in space is an enormous collection of stars?	*A galaxy*
8	What color is crimson?	*Deep red*
9	Is a bathyscaphe used to explore underground, under the sea, or outer space?	*Under the sea*
10	What is the remainder when 26 is divided by 3?	*Two*

Quiz 113
Question 7

Quiz 113
Question 3